JavaScript: From Beginner to Pro

A Step-by-Step Guide to Mastering JavaScript for Web Development

BOOZMAN RICHARD

BOOKER BLUNT

Table of Content

TABLE OF CONTENTS

INTRODUCTION

Mastering JavaScript for Web Development

Welcome to *Mastering JavaScript for Web Development*, a comprehensive guide that takes you on a journey through the powerful world of JavaScript and web development. Whether you are a beginner starting from scratch or an experienced developer looking to deepen your knowledge, this book is designed to provide you with the essential skills, tools, and techniques to become a proficient full-stack developer using JavaScript.

JavaScript has evolved from a simple scripting language for client-side interaction to a full-fledged programming language that powers the modern web. Today, JavaScript is at the core of web development, driving both front-end and back-end technologies, making it the most versatile language in the developer's toolkit. It is the language behind frameworks and libraries such as React, Angular, and Vue for building dynamic user interfaces, and Node.js for creating scalable server-side applications.

In this book, we dive deep into both **front-end** and **back-end** development using JavaScript, starting with the foundational concepts and progressing to advanced techniques and frameworks that are commonly used in the industry. By the end of this journey, you will be able to build fully functional, interactive web applications, manage databases, work with APIs, and optimize performance—all using JavaScript.

What You Will Learn

1. **JavaScript Fundamentals**:
   - Starting with the basics of JavaScript, you will learn about **variables, data types**, **operators**, **control structures**, **functions**, and **objects**. Understanding these fundamental concepts is essential as they lay the groundwork for more complex topics.
   - You will also be introduced to **ES6** and beyond, learning about modern features such as **arrow functions, classes, modules**, and **destructuring**.

2. **Client-Side Development with React**:
   - React is one of the most popular libraries for building dynamic, single-page applications

(SPAs). In this book, you will learn how to create interactive UIs using **React components, JSX, props**, and **state**.

o You will also explore **React hooks** such as `useState` and `useEffect` to manage state and side effects in functional components.

3. **Server-Side Development with Node.js and Express**:

o Learn how to use **Node.js** for server-side development and **Express**, a framework built on top of Node.js, to create web applications and RESTful APIs.

o You will gain an understanding of **routing**, **middleware**, and **RESTful principles**, and how to manage **HTTP requests and responses**.

4. **Working with Databases**:

o In full-stack web development, working with databases is essential. You will learn how to connect to and interact with **MongoDB**—a popular NoSQL database—using **Mongoose**.

o The book covers how to **create**, **read**, **update**, and **delete** data (CRUD operations) in MongoDB and how to structure your database for efficient data management.

5. **Building Full-Stack Applications**:
   o You will integrate your front-end (React) and back-end (Node.js/Express) to create full-stack applications. This includes handling **HTTP requests, working with APIs,** and **managing data flow** between the client and the server.

   o The book guides you through building a **CRUD application** with a full-stack architecture, providing you with hands-on experience in creating real-world applications.

6. **Optimizing and Debugging**:
   o As you develop your skills, you will also learn how to debug your JavaScript code using tools like **console logging, breakpoints,** and **browser DevTools.**

   o The book also covers **performance optimization techniques,** including how to improve the speed of your JavaScript-heavy web applications by reducing memory leaks, minimizing DOM manipulation, and optimizing network requests.

7. **Testing and Best Practices**:
   - **Unit testing** is a crucial part of ensuring the reliability and maintainability of your code. You will learn how to write tests for your JavaScript code using popular testing libraries like **Jest** and **Mocha**.
   - The book also introduces best practices in JavaScript development, including **code organization**, **modularization**, and **version control with Git**.

Real-World Examples

Throughout the book, you will engage with **real-world examples** that demonstrate how to apply JavaScript concepts in practical scenarios. For instance, you will:

- Build a **weather app** using React and external APIs, showcasing how to fetch and display data dynamically.
- Create a **RESTful API** using Node.js and Express, interacting with a MongoDB database for persistent storage.

CHAPTER 1

INTRODUCTION TO JAVASCRIPT

What is JavaScript? The Role of JavaScript in Web Development

JavaScript is a high-level, interpreted programming language that is primarily used for creating dynamic content on websites. It is one of the core technologies of the web, alongside HTML and CSS, making web pages interactive and engaging. While HTML provides the structure of the web page and CSS is responsible for styling, JavaScript enables dynamic behavior, allowing users to interact with the page.

Without JavaScript, a website would be static, meaning users would only be able to view content, without being able to perform tasks like submitting forms, loading new content without refreshing the page, or clicking buttons that trigger certain actions. JavaScript allows web developers to create interactive features like carousels, form validation, animations, and more.

In modern web development, JavaScript is used on both the client-side (in the user's browser) and the server-side (through environments like Node.js). This makes JavaScript a versatile language, essential for building web applications, websites, and even mobile applications.

- Develop a **full-stack application** with React for the front-end and Express for the back-end, demonstrating the integration of various technologies in a complete application.

These examples are designed to equip you with the skills necessary to build your own projects, whether you're creating small interactive apps or large-scale enterprise applications.

Who This Book is For

This book is intended for anyone who is eager to learn **JavaScript** and how to use it for web development. It's suitable for:

- **Beginners** who want to get started with JavaScript and web development.
- **Intermediate developers** who are familiar with JavaScript and want to learn how to build full-stack applications.
- **Experienced developers** looking to broaden their knowledge of modern JavaScript frameworks and libraries.

No prior knowledge of **React**, **Node.js**, or **Express** is required to get started. The book takes you step-by-step through the fundamentals, ensuring that you build a strong foundation before diving into more advanced topics.

What You Need to Know Before You Start

Before diving into the book, you should have a basic understanding of HTML, CSS, and JavaScript. If you're completely new to JavaScript, don't worry—the first few chapters of this book provide a detailed overview of the language's core concepts. As you move forward, the book progressively builds on these concepts, introducing more advanced tools and techniques in an accessible way.

Conclusion and Next Steps

By the end of this book, you will have a deep understanding of full-stack JavaScript development. You will be capable of:

- Building interactive user interfaces with **React**.
- Setting up servers and creating APIs with **Node.js** and **Express**.
- Working with databases using **MongoDB** and integrating it into your applications.

- Writing clean, maintainable code and optimizing your applications for performance.
- Testing your applications to ensure reliability and functionality.

The skills you acquire in this book will not only help you build powerful web applications but also prepare you for real-world web development challenges. Once you have mastered the core topics, the next step is to continue practicing and exploring more advanced topics like:

- **Authentication and authorization** with JWT or OAuth.
- **Real-time applications** using **WebSockets**.
- **State management** in React with tools like **Redux** or **Context API**.
- **Serverless architectures** and **GraphQL** for modern back-end development.

With the knowledge gained from this book, you will be well-equipped to take on a variety of web development projects, whether you're working solo or as part of a development team.

Welcome to your journey of becoming a **full-stack JavaScript developer**. The skills you will gain in this book are in high demand and will open up opportunities for you to create modern, dynamic web applications that meet the needs of today's users. Let's get started!

Basic Concepts: Variables, Data Types, and Operators

To begin writing JavaScript, you need to understand the core building blocks. These include variables, data types, and operators, which are fundamental to storing and manipulating data in your programs.

1. **Variables**: Variables are used to store values that can be used and manipulated throughout your program. In JavaScript, you can declare variables using `var`, `let`, or `const`:

   o `let`: Used to declare variables that can be reassigned later.

   o `const`: Used to declare variables whose values cannot be reassigned once set.

   o `var`: An older way of declaring variables, but generally avoided in modern JavaScript due to its scope limitations.

   ```javascript
   let age = 25; // A variable that holds a number
   const name = "John"; // A variable that holds a string (constant value)
   ```

2. **Data Types**: JavaScript supports several types of data, each used for different purposes:

- o **String**: A sequence of characters (e.g., `"Hello, World!"`).
- o **Number**: Numerical values (e.g., `42`, `3.14`).
- o **Boolean**: Represents true or false values (`true`, `false`).
- o **Undefined**: A variable that has been declared but not assigned a value.
- o **Null**: A special value that represents no value or object.
- o **Object**: A collection of key-value pairs used to store more complex data.
- o **Array**: A collection of ordered data values.

```javascript
let name = "Alice"; // string
let age = 30; // number
let isStudent = true; // boolean
```

3. **Operators**: Operators allow you to perform operations on variables and values:
   - o **Arithmetic Operators**: Used to perform mathematical calculations (`+`, `-`, `*`, `/`, `%`).
   - o **Comparison Operators**: Used to compare values (`==`, `!=`, `>`, `<`, `>=`, `<=`).
   - o **Logical Operators**: Used to combine boolean values (`&&`, `||`, `!`).

17

```javascript
javascript

let sum = 10 + 5; // Addition operator
let isAdult = age >= 18; // Comparison
operator
let isEligible = isStudent && age < 30; //
Logical operator
```

Real-World Example: Building Your First JavaScript Program

Now that you've learned the basics of JavaScript, it's time to build your first simple program. Let's create a small program that takes user input, processes it, and displays a result on the webpage.

Example: Simple Age Validator

This program will ask the user to enter their age, check if they are old enough to drive (18 or older), and then display a message based on their input.

```html
html

<!DOCTYPE html>
<html lang="en">
<head>
    <meta charset="UTF-8">
    <meta name="viewport" content="width=device-
width, initial-scale=1.0">
    <title>Age Validator</title>
</head>
```

```
<body>
    <h1>Age Validator</h1>
    <p>Enter your age:</p>
    <input type="text" id="ageInput">
    <button onclick="checkAge()">Submit</button>
    <p id="message"></p>

    <script>
        function checkAge() {
            // Get the input value from the user
            let                age               =
document.getElementById('ageInput').value;

            // Convert the input to a number (in
case the user enters a string)
            age = Number(age);

            // Check if the user is old enough to
drive
            if (age >= 18) {

document.getElementById('message').innerHTML   =
"You are old enough to drive!";
            } else {

document.getElementById('message').innerHTML   =
"Sorry, you are not old enough to drive.";
            }
        }
```

```
</script>
</body>
</html>
```

How it works:

1. The program prompts the user to enter their age in an input field.
2. The `checkAge()` function is called when the user clicks the submit button.
3. It retrieves the user's input, checks if it's 18 or older, and then displays an appropriate message on the page.

This example demonstrates how JavaScript can be used to interact with a webpage, gather user input, process it, and display the result dynamically.

CHAPTER 2

SETTING UP YOUR

DEVELOPMENT ENVIRONMENT

Installing Text Editors and Browsers

To start working with JavaScript, you need a reliable development environment. This includes a text editor for writing code and a web browser to view and test your code. Let's walk through the steps for setting up both.

1. **Text Editors**: A text editor is where you write your JavaScript code. While there are many options, the following are popular choices for web development:

     o **Visual Studio Code (VS Code)**: A free, open-source, and feature-rich text editor that provides powerful JavaScript support, including syntax highlighting, code suggestions, and debugging tools.

     ▪ **Installation**:

          ▪ Go to Visual Studio Code's website and download the version for your operating system.

21

- After installation, launch VS Code, and you're ready to start coding.
  - o **Sublime Text**: A lightweight, fast text editor. It's known for its simplicity and powerful extensions.
    - **Installation**: Download from Sublime Text's website, and follow the setup instructions.
  - o **Atom**: Another popular text editor developed by GitHub, known for being customizable and developer-friendly.
    - **Installation**: Download from Atom's website, and follow the setup instructions.

2. **Web Browsers**: Browsers allow you to view your web pages and test JavaScript in real-time. The most commonly used browsers are:
   - o **Google Chrome**: Offers powerful developer tools for debugging and testing JavaScript.
   - o **Mozilla Firefox**: Provides excellent developer tools, particularly useful for front-end development.
   - o **Microsoft Edge**: Built on Chromium (the same engine as Google Chrome), it offers similar developer tools.

Once installed, you'll use these browsers to test and see your JavaScript code in action. It's a good idea to use more than one browser for testing because each browser may render pages slightly differently.

Setting Up a Simple Web Development Environment

Now that you have your text editor and browser, let's set up a simple web development environment.

1. **Create a Project Folder**:
   o Start by creating a folder on your computer where you'll store all your JavaScript files. This will keep your projects organized.
   o For example, create a folder named `JavaScript_Project`.

2. **Create Your First HTML and JavaScript Files**:
   o Inside your project folder, create a new file named `index.html`. This will be the main HTML file for your web page.
   o Next, create a JavaScript file named `script.js`. This file will contain the JavaScript code that interacts with the HTML.

3. **Basic HTML Structure**:
   o Open `index.html` in your text editor and type the following HTML code:

html

```
<!DOCTYPE html>
<html lang="en">
<head>
    <meta charset="UTF-8">
    <meta                name="viewport"
content="width=device-width,      initial-
scale=1.0">
    <title>JavaScript Project</title>
</head>
<body>
    <h1>Welcome    to    My    JavaScript
Project</h1>
    <p id="message">This message will be
updated by JavaScript.</p>

    <!-- Link to the JavaScript file -->
    <script src="script.js"></script>
</body>
</html>
```

This simple HTML structure contains an <h1> header, a paragraph with an ID of "message," and a <script> tag linking to the script.js file.

4. **Add Some JavaScript**:

   o   Open script.js in your text editor and add the following code:

```
javascript

// JavaScript code to update the message
document.getElementById('message').innerH
TML = "Hello, JavaScript is working!";
```

This JavaScript code accesses the paragraph with the ID `message` and changes its text to "Hello, JavaScript is working!"

5. **View the Web Page**:

   o Open `index.html` in your web browser. You should see a page that says, "Welcome to My JavaScript Project," and below it, the message "Hello, JavaScript is working!" will appear.

   o If the text changes, your environment is properly set up, and your JavaScript is working!

Introduction to Browser Developer Tools

Browser developer tools are essential for testing, debugging, and optimizing your web pages. These tools are built into modern browsers like Google Chrome, Mozilla Firefox, and Microsoft Edge. Let's focus on **Google Chrome's Developer Tools**, but most browsers have similar features.

1. **Accessing Developer Tools**:

25

- o In Google Chrome, you can open the Developer Tools by right-clicking on the page and selecting **Inspect**, or by pressing `Ctrl+Shift+I` (Windows/Linux) or `Cmd+Option+I` (Mac).

- o This opens the Developer Tools panel, which is divided into several tabs: **Elements, Console, Network, Sources, Application**, and more.

2. **Using the Console**:

   - o The **Console** tab allows you to see any output from your JavaScript code and log errors or messages. For example, if you add a `console.log` statement in your JavaScript, it will appear here.

```javascript
console.log("JavaScript is working!");
```

   - o This will display the message `"JavaScript is working!"` in the console.

3. **Inspecting Elements**:

   - o The **Elements** tab shows the HTML structure of the page. You can click on elements to see their HTML code and styles. You can even modify the HTML and CSS directly in this panel to see live changes on your page.

4. **Debugging JavaScript**:

o The **Sources** tab allows you to set breakpoints in your JavaScript code and step through the code line by line. This is very useful for troubleshooting bugs and understanding how your code is executed.

o To set a breakpoint, open the **Sources** tab, find your `script.js` file, and click on the line number where you want the debugger to pause. Then refresh your page, and your code will pause at that line, allowing you to inspect variables and step through the code.

5. **Network Tab**:

o The **Network** tab shows all the requests made by the browser (like loading resources, APIs, etc.). It's helpful for seeing if your JavaScript is interacting correctly with APIs or loading resources as expected.

By using these developer tools, you can inspect your page, debug JavaScript, and optimize your web development process, all within your browser.

Summary

In this chapter, you've learned how to set up a basic web development environment, including installing a text editor and browser. You also learned how to create a simple web page with

HTML and JavaScript and test it in a browser. Lastly, you were introduced to browser developer tools, which will help you test, debug, and optimize your code more effectively as you advance in your JavaScript learning.

CHAPTER 3

JAVASCRIPT SYNTAX AND STRUCTURE

Writing Basic JavaScript: Syntax Rules, Structure, and Conventions

JavaScript, like any programming language, has specific syntax rules and conventions that you need to follow in order to write functional code. These rules govern how the code should be written, including how to declare variables, write functions, and structure your code logically.

1. **Statements**:
   - A statement is a single instruction that tells the computer what to do. Each statement ends with a semicolon (;). However, JavaScript does have **automatic semicolon insertion**, meaning that in many cases, the semicolon can be omitted, and JavaScript will insert it for you at the end of the statement. Still, it's considered best practice to include semicolons to avoid confusion or errors.

```javascript
let message = "Hello, world!"; // Correct:
semicolon used at the end
```

2. **Variables**:

   o Variables store data values that can change over time. In JavaScript, variables can be declared using `var`, `let`, or `const`.

      - `let` allows you to reassign the variable.
      - `const` is used when the variable value shouldn't change.
      - `var` is an older way of declaring variables and is now less commonly used.

   javascript

   ```javascript
   let name = "Alice"; // variable that can change
   const birthYear = 1995; // constant value
   ```

3. **Functions**:

   o Functions are blocks of code designed to perform a specific task. You can define a function using the `function` keyword, followed by the function name, parentheses, and curly braces that enclose the code block.

   javascript

   ```javascript
   function greet() {
     console.log("Hello, World!");
   ```

```
}
greet(); // Calls the function
```

4. **Comments**:
   - o Comments are used to explain code and are ignored by JavaScript during execution. There are two types of comments in JavaScript:
     - ▪ **Single-line comments**: Use `//` to comment a single line.
     - ▪ **Multi-line comments**: Use `/*` to start and `*/` to end a multi-line comment.

```javascript

// This is a single-line comment
/* This is a
   multi-line comment */
```

Understanding Semicolons, Braces, and Indentation

1. **Semicolons (;)**:
   - o A semicolon marks the end of a statement in JavaScript. While JavaScript often automatically inserts semicolons at the end of statements, it's still best practice to use them explicitly to avoid errors, especially in complex code.
2. **Braces ({ })**:
   - o Curly braces { } are used to define blocks of code, such as for functions, loops, and conditional

31

statements. Everything inside the braces will be considered as part of that block.

```
javascript
```

```javascript
if (age >= 18) {
  console.log("You are an adult.");
} else {
  console.log("You are a minor.");
}
```

3. **Indentation**:

   o Indentation helps to make the code more readable and organized. Each block of code inside functions, loops, and conditionals should be indented properly to show its hierarchy or relationship with other parts of the code.

   o It's a convention to use 2 or 4 spaces for indentation (some developers use tabs). Make sure to be consistent with your choice throughout the code.

```
javascript
```

```javascript
function checkAge(age) {
  if (age >= 18) {
    console.log("You can drive.");
  } else {
    console.log("You cannot drive.");
```

```
        }
    }
```

Real-World Example: Creating a Basic Interactive Webpage

Let's create a basic interactive webpage that changes the text on the page when a button is clicked. This example will demonstrate how to use JavaScript syntax, structure, semicolons, braces, and indentation to create a functional webpage.

Example: Click-to-Change Text Webpage

1. **HTML (index.html)**: The HTML structure will contain a button and a paragraph. When the button is clicked, the paragraph text will change using JavaScript.

    html

    ```html
    <!DOCTYPE html>
    <html lang="en">
    <head>
        <meta charset="UTF-8">
        <meta                name="viewport"
    content="width=device-width,      initial-
    scale=1.0">
        <title>Interactive Webpage</title>
    </head>
    <body>
        <h1>Welcome    to    the    Interactive
    Webpage</h1>
    ```

```
<p id="message">Click the button to
change this text.</p>
<button id="changeTextButton">Change
Text</button>

<!-- Link to the JavaScript file -->
<script src="script.js"></script>
</body>
</html>
```

2. **JavaScript (script.js)**: Now, let's write the JavaScript code to change the paragraph text when the button is clicked.

javascript

```
// Select the button and the paragraph by
their IDs
let               button               =
document.getElementById("changeTextButton
");
let              message               =
document.getElementById("message");

// Add an event listener to the button
button.addEventListener("click",
function() {
  // Change the text inside the paragraph
when the button is clicked
```

```
message.innerHTML = "The text has been
changed!";
});
```

How it works:

- o We first select the button and paragraph elements by their `id` attributes using `document.getElementById()`.
- o Then, we use `addEventListener()` to attach a `click` event to the button.
- o When the button is clicked, the `innerHTML` property of the paragraph is changed to "The text has been changed!"

Summary

In this chapter, you've learned the basic syntax and structure of JavaScript, including how to write statements, declare variables, and define functions. You also explored the importance of semicolons, braces, and proper indentation to keep code readable and functional. The real-world example of creating a basic interactive webpage demonstrated how to apply these concepts to build a simple but effective JavaScript-driven interaction on a webpage.

CHAPTER 4

WORKING WITH VARIABLES AND DATA TYPES

Primitive Data Types: Strings, Numbers, Booleans, Undefined, Null

In JavaScript, **data types** define what kind of data can be stored in a variable. The primitive data types are the building blocks of the language, and understanding them is essential for working with JavaScript. Let's look at the key primitive data types:

1. **String**:
    - A string is a sequence of characters enclosed in either single (') or double (") quotes. Strings can contain letters, numbers, symbols, and spaces.

```javascript
let greeting = "Hello, world!"; // A string
enclosed in double quotes
let name = 'Alice'; // A string enclosed in
single quotes
```

2. **Number**:
    - Numbers represent numeric values, either integers or floating-point numbers (decimals). In

JavaScript, there's no need to distinguish between integers and floating-point numbers; both are of the number type.

```javascript

let age = 25; // An integer
let price = 19.99; // A floating-point
number
```

3. **Boolean**:
    o A boolean represents one of two possible values: true or false. Booleans are used for conditional statements (like if/else) to check conditions.

```javascript

let isAdult = true; // Boolean value
representing true
let isStudent = false; // Boolean value
representing false
```

4. **Undefined**:
    o undefined is a special data type that means a variable has been declared, but hasn't been assigned a value. By default, JavaScript assigns the value undefined to uninitialized variables.

```
javascript
```

```
let color;
console.log(color); // Outputs: undefined
because 'color' hasn't been assigned a
value yet
```

5. **Null**:

   o   `null` is another special value in JavaScript that represents "no value" or "empty." It's different from `undefined`, which signifies an uninitialized variable, whereas `null` is explicitly assigned to indicate that a variable has no value.

```
javascript
```

```
let car = null; // Explicitly set to null,
meaning no car assigned
```

Variables: var, let, const

Variables are used to store data in JavaScript. There are three main ways to declare variables: `var`, `let`, and `const`. Each has its own characteristics:

1. **var**:

   o   `var` is the oldest way to declare variables. It has function scope (limited to the function it's declared in) and can be re-declared and updated.

38

It's generally avoided in modern JavaScript in favor of `let` and `const` due to potential scoping issues.

javascript

```
var x = 10;
x = 20; // Reassigning a value to 'x' works
fine
```

2. **let**:

o   `let` is the recommended way to declare variables in modern JavaScript. It has block scope, meaning it only exists within the block (e.g., a loop or if statement) where it is declared. It can be reassigned but cannot be redeclared within the same scope.

javascript

```
let age = 30; // Declare a variable
age = 35; // Reassigning a new value works
fine
```

3. **const**:

o   `const` is used to declare variables whose values should not change after they're set. Like `let`, it has block scope. However, you cannot reassign a value to a variable declared with `const`. This makes it suitable for values that need to stay constant.

```javascript
const PI = 3.14159; // PI is a constant value
// PI = 3.14; // This will throw an error because PI cannot be reassigned
```

Real-World Example: Simple Calculations and Data Handling

Let's apply what we've learned by creating a simple calculator that handles basic operations like addition, subtraction, multiplication, and division. We will use variables to store numbers, perform calculations, and display the results.

Example: A Simple Calculator

1. **HTML (index.html)**: We'll set up a basic webpage with input fields to enter numbers, buttons to trigger calculations, and a place to display the results.

```html
<!DOCTYPE html>
<html lang="en">
<head>
    <meta charset="UTF-8">
```

```
    <meta                    name="viewport"
content="width=device-width,        initial-
scale=1.0">
    <title>Simple Calculator</title>
</head>
<body>
    <h1>Simple Calculator</h1>
    <input      type="number"      id="num1"
placeholder="Enter first number">
    <input      type="number"      id="num2"
placeholder="Enter second number">
    <button
onclick="calculate()">Calculate</button>
    <p id="result">Result: </p>

    <!-- Link to the JavaScript file -->
    <script src="script.js"></script>
</body>
</html>
```

2. **JavaScript (script.js)**: We'll write JavaScript to retrieve the values from the input fields, perform a calculation based on those values, and display the result.

```javascript

function calculate() {
  // Retrieve values from the input fields
```

41

```javascript
    let          num1          =
document.getElementById('num1').value;
    let          num2          =
document.getElementById('num2').value;

    // Convert the input values to numbers
    num1 = Number(num1);
    num2 = Number(num2);

    // Check if the inputs are valid numbers
    if (isNaN(num1) || isNaN(num2)) {

document.getElementById('result').innerHT
ML = "Please enter valid numbers.";
        return;
    }

    // Perform the calculations
    let sum = num1 + num2;
    let difference = num1 - num2;
    let product = num1 * num2;
    let quotient = num1 / num2;

    // Display the results

document.getElementById('result').innerHT
ML = `
    Sum: ${sum}<br>
    Difference: ${difference}<br>
```

42

```
Product: ${product}<br>
Quotient: ${quotient}
    `;
}
```

How it works:

- When the user enters two numbers and clicks the "Calculate" button, the JavaScript function `calculate()` is triggered.
- The function retrieves the values from the input fields and converts them to numbers.
- The calculations for the sum, difference, product, and quotient are performed.
- Finally, the results are displayed on the webpage.

Summary

In this chapter, we covered the primitive data types in JavaScript—strings, numbers, booleans, undefined, and null. You also learned about variables and how to declare them using `var`, `let`, and `const`, each with its own purpose and scope rules. The real-world example of a simple calculator demonstrated how to work with variables, perform basic mathematical operations, and display results dynamically on a webpage. These concepts form the foundation of JavaScript, and you'll use them repeatedly as you build more complex applications.

CHAPTER 5

CONTROL STRUCTURES (CONDITIONALS AND LOOPS)

Control structures in JavaScript allow you to control the flow of your program based on conditions or by repeating certain operations. These structures include conditionals like `if`, `else`, and `switch` statements, and loops such as `for`, `while`, and `do-while`. Understanding how to use these will enable you to create more dynamic and interactive programs.

If, Else, and Switch Statements

1. **If Statement**:
   - The `if` statement is used to execute a block of code only if a specified condition is true. If the condition evaluates to false, the block of code inside the `if` statement will be skipped.

```javascript
let age = 20;
if (age >= 18) {
  console.log("You are an adult.");
}
```

In this example, the message "You are an adult" will be logged because the condition `age >= 18` is true.

2. **Else Statement**:

   o The `else` statement is used in conjunction with an `if` statement. It provides an alternative block of code to run when the condition in the `if` statement evaluates to false.

```javascript
let age = 16;
if (age >= 18) {
  console.log("You are an adult.");
} else {
  console.log("You are a minor.");
}
```

Since the condition `age >= 18` is false, the message "You are a minor" will be logged.

3. **Else If Statement**:

   o If you have multiple conditions to check, you can use `else if` to test additional conditions.

```javascript
let age = 25;
if (age < 13) {
```

```
    console.log("You are a child.");
} else if (age < 20) {
    console.log("You are a teenager.");
} else {
    console.log("You are an adult.");
}
```

In this example, the message "You are an adult" will be logged because the age is greater than 19.

4. **Switch Statement**:

   o The `switch` statement is an alternative to multiple `if` and `else if` statements when you need to check a variable against multiple values. It's often used when you have many conditions that depend on the same variable.

```
javascript

let day = 2;
switch (day) {
  case 1:
    console.log("Sunday");
    break;
  case 2:
    console.log("Monday");
    break;
  case 3:
    console.log("Tuesday");
```

```
    break;
  default:
    console.log("Invalid day");
}
```

The `switch` statement checks the value of `day` and matches it to one of the `case` values. In this case, since `day = 2`, the message "Monday" will be logged. The `break` statement is used to exit the switch block after the matching case is executed.

Loops: For, While, Do-While

1. **For Loop**:
   o A `for` loop is used when you know how many times you need to repeat a block of code. It's often used for iterating over arrays or running a block of code a specific number of times.

```javascript
javascript

for (let i = 0; i < 5; i++) {
  console.log(i);
}
```

This loop will log numbers from 0 to 4. The three parts of the loop are:

- o **Initialization**: `let i = 0` (sets the starting value)
- o **Condition**: `i < 5` (checks if the loop should continue)
- o **Increment**: `i++` (increments the value of `i` after each iteration)

2. **While Loop**:

- o A `while` loop is used when you want to repeat a block of code as long as a certain condition is true. It is particularly useful when you don't know the number of iterations in advance.

```javascript
let i = 0;
while (i < 5) {
  console.log(i);
  i++;
}
```

This loop will also log numbers from 0 to 4. The loop continues running as long as the condition `i < 5` is true.

3. **Do-While Loop**:

- o The `do-while` loop is similar to the `while` loop, but it guarantees that the code inside the loop will run at least once, regardless of whether the condition is true or false.

48

```javascript
let i = 0;
do {
  console.log(i);
  i++;
} while (i < 5);
```

This loop will behave the same as the `while` loop in this example, but it ensures that the code block is executed at least once before the condition is checked.

Real-World Example: Creating a Number Guessing Game

Let's apply the concepts of conditionals and loops by creating a simple **Number Guessing Game**. In this game, the user has to guess a number between 1 and 10, and the program will tell them if their guess is too high, too low, or correct. The game will loop until the user guesses correctly.

Example: Number Guessing Game

1. **HTML (index.html)**: We'll create a basic webpage with an input field to enter a guess and a button to submit it.

```html
<!DOCTYPE html>
<html lang="en">
```

```html
<head>
    <meta charset="UTF-8">
    <meta                    name="viewport"
content="width=device-width,        initial-
scale=1.0">
    <title>Number Guessing Game</title>
</head>
<body>
    <h1>Guess   the   Number   Between   1   and
10</h1>
    <input    type="number"    id="guess"
placeholder="Enter your guess">
    <button
onclick="guessNumber()">Submit</button>
    <p id="message"></p>

    <script src="script.js"></script>
</body>
</html>
```

2. **JavaScript (script.js)**: Now we'll write the JavaScript code for the guessing game. We'll generate a random number, compare it with the user's guess, and provide feedback.

```javascript
// Generate a random number between 1 and
10
```

```javascript
let                randomNumber              =
Math.floor(Math.random() * 10) + 1;
let attempts = 0;

function guessNumber() {
  // Get the user's guess
  let                userGuess                =
document.getElementById('guess').value;
  attempts++;


  // Check if the guess is correct, too
high, or too low
  if (userGuess == randomNumber) {

document.getElementById('message').innerH
TML = `Correct! You guessed the number in
${attempts} attempts.`;
  } else if (userGuess < randomNumber) {

document.getElementById('message').innerH
TML = "Too low! Try again.";
  } else {

document.getElementById('message').innerH
TML = "Too high! Try again.";
  }
}
```

How it works:

- When the user enters a guess and clicks the "Submit" button, the `guessNumber()` function is called.
- The function compares the user's guess to the randomly generated number and provides feedback based on whether the guess is too high, too low, or correct.
- The game continues until the user guesses correctly.

Summary

In this chapter, we learned how to use control structures such as `if`, `else`, `else if`, and `switch` statements to make decisions in our programs. We also explored how to use loops—`for`, `while`, and `do-while`—to repeat actions multiple times. These control structures are essential for creating dynamic and interactive applications. The real-world example of a number guessing game demonstrated how to combine these concepts to build an engaging JavaScript program.

CHAPTER 6

FUNCTIONS IN JAVASCRIPT

Defining and Calling Functions

Functions are one of the most important building blocks in JavaScript. A function is a block of code designed to perform a specific task. Functions allow you to reuse code, making your programs more efficient and easier to maintain.

1. **Defining a Function**:
   - o Functions in JavaScript are defined using the `function` keyword, followed by the function name, a pair of parentheses `()`, and curly braces `{}` that enclose the code to be executed.

```javascript
function greet() {
  console.log("Hello, world!");
}
```

In this example, the function `greet()` simply logs "Hello, world!" to the console. However, the function doesn't do anything until it is called.

2. **Calling a Function**:

53

- o Once a function is defined, you can call it by using its name followed by parentheses.

```javascript
greet(); // Calls the greet function and prints "Hello, world!"
```

Calling the function causes the code inside it to execute. In this case, the message `"Hello, world!"` is printed in the console.

Function Parameters and Return Values

1. **Function Parameters**:
   - o Functions can accept **parameters**, which are values passed into the function when it is called. These parameters are used to perform calculations or operations within the function.
   - o You define parameters by placing them inside the parentheses when declaring the function. You can then use these parameters as variables within the function.

```javascript
function greetPerson(name) {
  console.log("Hello, " + name + "!");
}
```

```
greetPerson("Alice"); // Outputs: "Hello,
Alice!"
```

In this example, the function `greetPerson` takes a parameter `name` and uses it to print a personalized greeting.

2. **Return Values**:

   o Functions can also return a value using the `return` keyword. This allows the function to produce a result that can be used elsewhere in the program.

```javascript
function addNumbers(a, b) {
  return a + b;
}

let sum = addNumbers(5, 3);
console.log(sum); // Outputs: 8
```

In this case, the function `addNumbers` accepts two parameters a and b, adds them together, and returns the result. The returned value is stored in the variable `sum` and logged to the console.

Real-World Example: Building a Basic Calculator

Let's put these concepts into practice by creating a simple calculator that can perform basic arithmetic operations like addition, subtraction, multiplication, and division. We'll use functions to handle each operation, making the code modular and reusable.

Example: Basic Calculator

1. **HTML (index.html)**: We will set up a simple webpage with buttons for each arithmetic operation, an input field to enter numbers, and a place to display the result.

html

```
<!DOCTYPE html>
<html lang="en">
<head>
    <meta charset="UTF-8">
    <meta                     name="viewport"
content="width=device-width,      initial-
scale=1.0">
    <title>Basic Calculator</title>
</head>
<body>
    <h1>Basic Calculator</h1>
    <input    type="number"    id="num1"
placeholder="Enter first number">
```

```
    <input      type="number"     id="num2"
placeholder="Enter second number">
    <br>
    <button onclick="add()">Add</button>
    <button
onclick="subtract()">Subtract</button>
    <button
onclick="multiply()">Multiply</button>
    <button
onclick="divide()">Divide</button>
    <p id="result">Result: </p>

    <script src="script.js"></script>
</body>
</html>
```

2. **JavaScript (script.js)**: Now let's define functions for each operation and link them to the buttons on the webpage.

```
javascript

// Function to add two numbers
function add() {
    let              num1              =
Number(document.getElementById('num1').va
lue);
```

```
    let                num2              =
Number(document.getElementById('num2').va
lue);
    let result = num1 + num2;

document.getElementById('result').innerHT
ML = "Result: " + result;
    }

    // Function to subtract two numbers
    function subtract() {
    let                num1              =
Number(document.getElementById('num1').va
lue);
    let                num2              =
Number(document.getElementById('num2').va
lue);
    let result = num1 - num2;

document.getElementById('result').innerHT
ML = "Result: " + result;
    }

    // Function to multiply two numbers
    function multiply() {
    let                num1              =
Number(document.getElementById('num1').va
lue);
```

```javascript
    let             num2             =
Number(document.getElementById('num2').va
lue);
    let result = num1 * num2;

document.getElementById('result').innerHT
ML = "Result: " + result;
    }


// Function to divide two numbers
function divide() {
    let             num1             =
Number(document.getElementById('num1').va
lue);
    let             num2             =
Number(document.getElementById('num2').va
lue);
    if (num2 === 0) {

document.getElementById('result').innerHT
ML = "Error: Division by zero is not
allowed!";
    } else {
        let result = num1 / num2;

document.getElementById('result').innerHT
ML = "Result: " + result;
    }
}
```

How it works:

- When the user enters two numbers and clicks one of the operation buttons (Add, Subtract, Multiply, or Divide), the corresponding function is called.
- Each function retrieves the values from the input fields using `document.getElementById('num1').value` and `document.getElementById('num2').value`.
- The function then performs the appropriate arithmetic operation, stores the result in a variable, and updates the result on the webpage.

Handling Division by Zero:

- The `divide()` function includes a check to prevent division by zero. If `num2` is zero, the function displays an error message instead of attempting to divide.

Summary

In this chapter, we learned how to define and call functions in JavaScript. Functions allow us to group blocks of code that can be reused, making our programs more efficient. We also explored how to pass parameters to functions and how to return values from them. The real-world example of a basic calculator demonstrated how to use functions to handle user input, perform arithmetic operations, and display the results dynamically on a webpage.

Understanding functions is crucial, as they are the foundation for more complex logic and operations in JavaScript.

CHAPTER 7

UNDERSTANDING OBJECTS AND ARRAYS

In JavaScript, objects and arrays are used to store and manage data in more complex ways. These structures allow you to work with collections of data efficiently. This chapter will help you understand how to create and manipulate objects and arrays, and how to use them to store and manage data in real-world applications.

Objects: Properties and Methods

1. **What is an Object?**

   o   An object in JavaScript is a collection of key-value pairs, where the keys are called **properties** and the values can be any data type. Objects are used to represent real-world entities, such as a person, a car, or a book.

```javascript
let person = {
  name: "Alice",
  age: 25,
```

```
    isStudent: true
};
```

In this example, the `person` object has three properties: `name`, `age`, and `isStudent`.

2. **Accessing Object Properties**:
    o   You can access the properties of an object using dot notation or bracket notation.

    ```javascript
    console.log(person.name);    //    Outputs:
    Alice
    console.log(person["age"]); // Outputs: 25
    ```

3. **Modifying Object Properties**:
    o   You can modify the value of an existing property by using dot notation or bracket notation.

    ```javascript
    person.age = 26; // Modifying using dot
    notation
    person["isStudent"] = false; // Modifying
    using bracket notation
    console.log(person.age); // Outputs: 26
    ```

4. **Adding and Deleting Properties**:

o You can add new properties to an object, or delete existing ones using the `delete` keyword.

javascript

```
person.city = "New York"; // Adding a new
property
delete person.isStudent; // Deleting a
property
console.log(person.city); // Outputs: New
York
```

5. **Methods in Objects**:

   o Objects can also contain methods, which are functions that are associated with the object. These methods can perform operations on the object's properties.

javascript

```
let person = {
  name: "Alice",
  age: 25,
  greet: function() {
    console.log("Hello, " + this.name);
  }
};
```

```
person.greet(); // Outputs: Hello, Alice
```

In this example, the `greet` method uses the `this` keyword to refer to the current object (`person`), allowing it to access the `name` property and print a greeting.

Arrays: Creation, Manipulation, and Methods

1. **What is an Array?**
   - An array is an ordered collection of data, where each item can be accessed by its **index** (starting from 0). Arrays can store values of any data type, including strings, numbers, and objects.

   javascript

   ```javascript
   let fruits = ["apple", "banana", "cherry"];
   ```

2. **Accessing Array Elements**:
   - You can access array elements by using their index number.

   javascript

   ```javascript
   console.log(fruits[0]); // Outputs: apple
   ```

3. **Modifying Array Elements**:
   - You can change the value of an array element by referring to its index.

   javascript

```
fruits[1] = "orange"; // Changing the
second element
console.log(fruits); // Outputs: ["apple",
"orange", "cherry"]
```

4. **Array Methods**:

   o JavaScript arrays come with built-in methods that allow you to manipulate data. Some commonly used methods include:

   - **push()**: Adds one or more elements to the end of an array.
   - **pop()**: Removes the last element from an array.
   - **shift()**: Removes the first element from an array.
   - **unshift()**: Adds one or more elements to the beginning of an array.
   - **concat()**: Merges two or more arrays.
   - **forEach()**: Iterates over each element in the array.

   Example:

```
javascript
```

```
fruits.push("grape"); // Adds 'grape' to
the end of the array
```

```
console.log(fruits); // Outputs: ["apple",
"orange", "cherry", "grape"]

fruits.pop(); // Removes the last element
console.log(fruits); // Outputs: ["apple",
"orange", "cherry"]

fruits.forEach(function(fruit) {
  console.log(fruit); // Prints each fruit
in the array
});
```

5. **Array Length**:

   o The `length` property returns the number of elements in an array.

   ```
   javascript
   ```

   ```
   console.log(fruits.length); // Outputs: 3
   ```

Real-World Example: Storing and Managing User Data

Let's put these concepts into practice by creating an object to store user information, such as name, age, and email, and an array to store multiple users. We'll also create functions to add new users and display their information.

Example: Storing and Managing User Data

1. **HTML (index.html)**: Set up a simple webpage to interact with user data.

html

```html
<!DOCTYPE html>
<html lang="en">
<head>
    <meta charset="UTF-8">
    <meta                    name="viewport"
content="width=device-width,       initial-
scale=1.0">
    <title>User Management</title>
</head>
<body>
    <h1>User Management</h1>
    <input       type="text"       id="name"
placeholder="Enter name">
    <input       type="number"       id="age"
placeholder="Enter age">
    <input       type="email"       id="email"
placeholder="Enter email">
    <button       onclick="addUser()">Add
User</button>
    <h2>All Users:</h2>
    <ul id="userList"></ul>

    <script src="script.js"></script>
</body>
```

```
</html>
```

2. **JavaScript (script.js)**: Now, let's define functions to store user data in an object and manage it in an array.

```javascript
let users = []; // Array to store user
objects

// Function to add a new user
function addUser() {
    let           name           =
document.getElementById("name").value;
    let           age            =
document.getElementById("age").value;
    let           email          =
document.getElementById("email").value;

    // Create a user object
    let user = {
      name: name,
      age: age,
      email: email
    };

    // Add the user object to the users array
    users.push(user);

    // Display the updated list of users
```

```
    displayUsers();
}


// Function to display all users
function displayUsers() {
    let              userList              =
document.getElementById("userList");
    userList.innerHTML = "";  // Clear the
current list

    // Loop through the users array and
display each user's information
    users.forEach(function(user) {
        let              listItem              =
document.createElement("li");
        listItem.innerHTML       =       `Name:
${user.name},   Age:   ${user.age},   Email:
${user.email}`;
        userList.appendChild(listItem);
    });
}
```

How it works:

- The addUser function retrieves the user input from the
  input fields, creates a user object, and adds it to the
  users array.

- The `displayUsers` function loops through the `users` array and displays each user's information in a list on the webpage.

- Every time a new user is added, the list is updated and displayed on the page.

Summary

In this chapter, we explored how to work with objects and arrays in JavaScript. Objects allow you to store collections of key-value pairs, and arrays let you store ordered collections of data. We discussed object properties and methods, how to create and manipulate arrays, and the various array methods available for data manipulation. The real-world example of storing and managing user data demonstrated how to use objects and arrays to manage complex data efficiently, making your JavaScript programs more practical and dynamic.

CHAPTER 8

UNDERSTANDING SCOPE AND CLOSURES

In JavaScript, **scope** and **closures** are important concepts for controlling the visibility and lifetime of variables. Understanding how these work will help you write more efficient, secure, and organized code. This chapter explains **local** and **global** scope, how **closures** function, and a real-world example of using closures to handle private data.

Local vs Global Scope

1. **Global Scope**:
   - A variable declared outside of any function is in **global scope**. It can be accessed and modified from anywhere in your code, including inside functions.
   - Global variables are accessible throughout your entire program, which can be helpful but also risky, as they can easily be overwritten or cause unexpected behavior if not handled carefully.

   javascript

```
let globalVar = "I'm a global variable"; //
Declared in global scope

function greet() {
  console.log(globalVar); // Can access
globalVar because it's in global scope
}

greet(); // Outputs: "I'm a global
variable"
```

2. **Local Scope**:

   o   A variable declared inside a function is in **local scope**. It can only be accessed and modified within that function. Once the function execution is completed, the local variable is no longer accessible.

```
javascript

function greet() {
  let localVar = "I'm a local variable"; //
Declared in local scope
  console.log(localVar); // Can access
localVar because it's in the same function
}

greet(); // Outputs: "I'm a local variable"
```

```
//   console.log(localVar);   //   Error:
localVar is not defined (it's out of scope)
```

3. **Function Scope**:

   o Variables declared with `var` are function-scoped, meaning they can be accessed anywhere within the function in which they are declared, but not outside of it.

```javascript
function example() {
  var localVar = "I'm function-scoped"; //
Declared with var
  console.log(localVar); // Outputs: "I'm
function-scoped"
}

example();
//   console.log(localVar);   //   Error:
localVar is not defined
```

4. **Block Scope**:

   o Variables declared with `let` and `const` are block-scoped. This means they are only accessible within the block (e.g., inside a loop or an `if` statement) where they are declared.

```javascript
javascript
```

```
if (true) {
  let blockVar = "I'm block-scoped";
  console.log(blockVar); // Outputs: "I'm
block-scoped"
}

// console.log(blockVar); // Error:
blockVar is not defined
```

Closures and How They Work in JavaScript

1. **What is a Closure?**
   o A **closure** in JavaScript is a function that "remembers" and can access variables from its outer (enclosing) function even after the outer function has finished execution.
   o Closures allow functions to have access to the scope in which they were created, not just the scope in which they are executed.

2. **How Closures Work**:
   o A closure occurs when a function is defined inside another function and the inner function references variables from the outer function. Even though the outer function has completed execution, the inner function still retains access to the outer function's variables.

```
javascript
```

```
function outer() {
  let outerVar = "I'm from the outer
function"; // Outer function's variable

  function inner() {
    console.log(outerVar);    //    Inner
function  accessing  outer  function's
variable
  }

  return inner; // Returning the inner
function, which forms a closure
}

let closureFunc = outer(); // Call outer
function and get the inner function
closureFunc(); // Outputs: "I'm from the
outer function"
```

In this example:

- o The `inner` function is returned from the `outer` function.
- o Even after `outer()` finishes execution, the `inner()` function retains access to `outerVar` through the closure.

3. **Practical Use of Closures**:

o Closures are commonly used to create private variables and encapsulate functionality. This allows you to control the accessibility of variables, ensuring that some data remains hidden from the outside world but still accessible to specific functions.

Real-World Example: Handling Private Data with Closures

One common use case for closures is **creating private data**. JavaScript does not have a built-in way to make variables truly private, but closures allow us to simulate private data by keeping it inaccessible from outside the function. This concept is used in **data encapsulation**, where only specific methods can access or modify private data.

Example: Creating a Bank Account with a Private Balance

We'll use closures to create a simple bank account with a private balance that can only be modified by certain functions.

1. **HTML (index.html)**: Create a simple webpage to interact with the bank account.

```html
```

```html
<!DOCTYPE html>
<html lang="en">
```

```
<head>
    <meta charset="UTF-8">
    <meta                    name="viewport"
content="width=device-width,        initial-
scale=1.0">
    <title>Bank Account</title>
</head>
<body>
    <h1>Bank Account</h1>
    <p id="balance">Balance: $0</p>
    <button onclick="deposit(100)">Deposit
$100</button>
    <button
onclick="withdraw(50)">Withdraw
$50</button>

    <script src="script.js"></script>
</body>
</html>
```

2. **JavaScript (script.js)**: Use closures to create a private `balance` variable that can only be modified by specific methods.

```javascript
function createBankAccount() {
  let balance = 0; // Private balance
variable
```

78

```
// Deposit function that increases the
balance
function deposit(amount) {
  if (amount > 0) {
    balance += amount;
    updateBalance();
  }
}


// Withdraw function that decreases the
balance
function withdraw(amount) {
  if (amount > 0 && amount <= balance) {
    balance -= amount;
    updateBalance();
  } else {
    console.log("Insufficient funds");
  }
}


// Function to update and display the
balance
function updateBalance() {

document.getElementById("balance").innerT
ext = `Balance: $${balance}`;
  }
```

```
  // Expose only the deposit and withdraw
methods, keeping balance private
  return {
    deposit: deposit,
    withdraw: withdraw
  };
}


// Create a new bank account instance
let account = createBankAccount();


// Global functions to interact with the
account
function deposit(amount) {
  account.deposit(amount); // Call deposit
method
}


function withdraw(amount) {
  account.withdraw(amount);      //     Call
withdraw method
}
```

How it works:

- The `createBankAccount` function creates a closure, where the `balance` variable is private and inaccessible from the outside.

- The `deposit` and `withdraw` functions are returned by `createBankAccount` and can interact with the `balance`. These functions are the only way to modify or view the balance.
- The balance is updated using the `updateBalance` function, which is also inside the closure.

This example demonstrates how closures can be used to encapsulate private data and expose only the necessary methods to interact with that data, ensuring that the internal state (the balance) is protected from direct access.

Summary

In this chapter, we explored the concepts of **scope** and **closures** in JavaScript. Local and global scope determine the accessibility of variables, and closures allow inner functions to retain access to variables from their outer functions even after the outer function has finished executing. We also saw how closures can be used in real-world applications, such as managing private data, to control access to sensitive information. By using closures, you can create more secure, modular, and efficient JavaScript code.

CHAPTER 9

THE 'THIS' KEYWORD

In JavaScript, the `this` keyword is one of the most crucial concepts to understand. It refers to the **context** in which a function or method is called and helps JavaScript determine which object or scope the function belongs to. This chapter will explain how `this` works in different contexts, the difference between arrow functions and traditional functions, and provide a real-world example of using `this` to implement object methods.

Understanding the Context of 'this' in Functions and Objects

1. **The `this` Keyword in Global Scope**:
   - In the global execution context (outside of any functions or objects), `this` refers to the **global object**. In a browser, the global object is the `window` object.

```javascript
console.log(this); // In a browser, this
logs the window object
```

   - However, in strict mode (`'use strict';`), `this` will be `undefined` in the global scope.

2. **The `this` Keyword in Functions**:

   o When a function is called, `this` refers to the **global object** in non-strict mode. In strict mode, `this` will be `undefined`.

```javascript
function example() {
  console.log(this);   // In non-strict
mode, logs the global object (e.g., window
in a browser)
}

example();
```

   o If a function is called as a method of an object, `this` refers to the **object** from which the function was called.

3. **The `this` Keyword in Objects**:

   o When a function is defined as a method of an object, `this` refers to the **object** itself.

```javascript
let person = {
  name: "Alice",
  greet: function() {
    console.log("Hello, " + this.name); //
'this' refers to the person object
```

```
    }
};
```

```
person.greet(); // Outputs: "Hello, Alice"
```

- o In this example, `this.name` refers to the `name` property of the `person` object.

4. **The `this` Keyword in Event Handlers**:
   - o When `this` is used inside an event handler, it refers to the **element** that triggered the event.

javascript

```
let                    button                    =
document.querySelector("button");

button.addEventListener("click",
function() {
   console.log(this); // 'this' refers to
the button element
});
```

- o In this case, `this` refers to the `button` element that was clicked, not the global object.

Arrow Functions vs Traditional Functions

1. **Arrow Functions**:

84

- o Arrow functions have a different behavior when it comes to the `this` keyword. In an arrow function, `this` is **lexically bound**, meaning that `this` retains the value of the `this` from the surrounding context (the place where the arrow function was defined). Arrow functions do not have their own `this` context.

```javascript
let person = {
  name: "Alice",
  greet: () => {
    console.log("Hello, " + this.name); // 'this' does not refer to the person object in arrow function
  }
};

person.greet();   //   Outputs:   "Hello, undefined"
```

- o In the example above, the arrow function does not work as expected because `this` refers to the **global object**, not the `person` object.

2. **Traditional Functions**:
  - o Traditional functions, on the other hand, **bind their own `this`** based on how they are called.

85

When a traditional function is used as a method of an object, `this` refers to the object.

```javascript
let person = {
  name: "Alice",
  greet: function() {
    console.log("Hello, " + this.name); // 'this' correctly refers to the person object
  }
};

person.greet(); // Outputs: "Hello, Alice"
```

- o In this case, `this` inside the traditional function correctly refers to the `person` object.

3. **Arrow Function and `this` Binding**:
   - o Arrow functions inherit `this` from their surrounding context and don't have their own `this`. They are great for situations where you want to retain the context of `this` from the surrounding scope (for example, inside event handlers, callbacks, or timers).

```javascript
```

```javascript
function Timer() {
  this.seconds = 0;
  setInterval(() => {
    this.seconds++; // 'this' refers to the
Timer object, not the global object
    console.log(this.seconds);
  }, 1000);
}


let timer = new Timer(); // Outputs: 1, 2,
3, ... every second
```

- o In this example, the arrow function allows this.seconds to correctly refer to the Timer object, even though it's inside the setInterval callback.

Real-World Example: Implementing Object Methods

In this example, we'll create an object representing a **car**, and we'll use the this keyword to implement methods for starting the car and displaying its details.

Example: Car Object with Methods

1. **JavaScript (script.js)**:

```
javascript
```

87

```javascript
let car = {
  make: "Toyota",
  model: "Camry",
  year: 2021,
  start: function() {
    console.log(this.make    +    "    "    +
this.model + " is now running.");
  },
  displayDetails: function() {
    console.log("Car Details:");
    console.log("Make: " + this.make);
    console.log("Model: " + this.model);
    console.log("Year: " + this.year);
  }
};

// Starting the car
car.start(); // Outputs: "Toyota Camry is
now running."

// Displaying the car details
car.displayDetails();
// Outputs:
// Car Details:
// Make: Toyota
// Model: Camry
// Year: 2021
```

2. **How it works**:

- o The start method uses this to refer to the car object, accessing the make and model properties.
- o The displayDetails method also uses this to print the car's details.
- o When these methods are called on the car object, this correctly refers to the car object, allowing us to access its properties.

3. **Using Arrow Functions in Objects**:
   - o To demonstrate the difference with arrow functions, let's see how using an arrow function would affect the behavior of the start method:

```javascript
let car = {
  make: "Toyota",
  model: "Camry",
  year: 2021,
  start: () => {
    console.log(this.make   +   "   "   +
this.model + " is now running.");
  }
};


car.start();   //   Outputs:   "undefined
undefined is now running."
```

o In this case, because the `start` method is an arrow function, `this` does not refer to the `car` object. Instead, it refers to the global object (or `undefined` in strict mode), which is why `this.make` and `this.model` are both `undefined`.

Summary

In this chapter, we explored how the `this` keyword works in JavaScript and how its behavior differs between traditional functions and arrow functions. The `this` keyword is used to reference the object or context in which a function is called. In traditional functions, `this` refers to the object from which the function was called, while in arrow functions, `this` is lexically bound to the surrounding context. We also saw a real-world example of implementing object methods using `this` to manage and interact with an object's properties, which demonstrates the practical use of `this` in real applications.

CHAPTER 10

ASYNCHRONOUS JAVASCRIPT (CALLBACKS AND PROMISES)

Asynchronous programming is a key feature of JavaScript that allows your program to perform non-blocking operations, such as fetching data from a server or reading files, without freezing the user interface or other tasks. This chapter will introduce asynchronous programming in JavaScript, explain how to use callbacks and promises to manage asynchronous tasks, and provide a real-world example of making an API call with promises.

Introduction to Asynchronous Programming

In traditional (synchronous) programming, each operation is executed one after the other. When one task is being processed, others must wait for it to finish. This can create performance issues, especially when working with tasks like fetching data over the network, reading large files, or performing lengthy calculations.

Asynchronous programming allows tasks to be executed concurrently, meaning that while one task is running (like fetching data from a server), other tasks can continue without waiting for the first one to complete. This helps improve the performance of web applications and ensures the user interface remains responsive.

In JavaScript, asynchronous operations are typically handled using **callbacks**, **promises**, or **async/await** (covered in later chapters). The most common use case for asynchronous programming is interacting with web APIs to fetch data.

Callbacks: Handling Asynchronous Tasks

A **callback** is a function that is passed as an argument to another function and is executed once the asynchronous operation is complete. Callbacks are commonly used in JavaScript to handle the results of asynchronous tasks.

1. **Basic Callback Example**:
   o   Here's an example of a basic callback function:

```javascript
function fetchData(callback) {
  setTimeout(function() {
    console.log("Data      fetched      from
server.");
    callback("Data is ready"); // Calling
the callback function after task is done
  }, 2000); // Simulating an asynchronous
task with setTimeout
```

92

```
}

function processData(message) {
  console.log(message);  // Handling the
result of the asynchronous task
}

fetchData(processData);  // Fetching data
and passing the processData function as a
callback
```

How it works:

- o The `fetchData` function simulates an asynchronous operation (like fetching data from a server) using `setTimeout`.
- o Once the operation is complete, it calls the `callback` function (in this case, `processData`), passing the result ("Data is ready") to the callback.
- o The `processData` function handles the result by logging it to the console.

2. **Callback Hell**:
   - o When you have multiple nested callbacks, the code can become difficult to read and maintain. This is often referred to as **callback hell**. Here's an example:

```
javascript

fetchData(function(data) {
  processData(data, function(result) {
    saveData(result, function(saved) {
      console.log("Data          saved
successfully.");
    });
  });
});
```

o   As you can see, nested callbacks can quickly become messy and hard to manage. This is one of the main reasons promises were introduced.

Promises: Managing Asynchronous Operations

A **promise** is an object that represents the eventual completion or failure of an asynchronous operation. Promises allow you to handle asynchronous operations in a more organized way, reducing the problems associated with callback hell.

1.   **What is a Promise?**

o   A promise is in one of three states:

- **Pending**: The operation is still ongoing.
- **Resolved (Fulfilled)**: The operation completed successfully.

- **Rejected**: The operation failed, usually due to an error.

A promise provides methods to handle these states:

o `then()`: Used to specify what should happen when the promise is resolved (successful completion).

o `catch()`: Used to specify what should happen if the promise is rejected (failure).

2. **Creating and Using a Promise**:

javascript

```javascript
function fetchData() {
  return new Promise((resolve, reject) =>
{
    let success = true; // Simulate a
successful or failed operation
    setTimeout(function() {
      if (success) {
        resolve("Data          fetched
successfully.");
      } else {
        reject("Error fetching data.");
      }
    }, 2000);
  });
}
```

```
fetchData()
  .then(result => {
    console.log(result); // Handle success
  })
  .catch(error => {
    console.log(error); // Handle failure
  });
```

How it works:

- o `fetchData` returns a promise. Inside the promise, we simulate an asynchronous task (e.g., fetching data) using `setTimeout`.
- o If the operation is successful, we call `resolve()` to indicate that the promise has been fulfilled.
- o If something goes wrong, we call `reject()` to indicate that the promise has been rejected.
- o We use `then()` to handle a successful operation and `catch()` to handle any errors.

3. **Chaining Promises**:
   - o You can chain multiple promises to handle a sequence of asynchronous operations.

```
javascript
```

```
fetchData()
  .then(result => {
```

```
console.log(result);
return    processData(result);    //
Returning a new promise
})
.then(processedData => {
console.log(processedData);
})
.catch(error => {
console.log(error);
});
```

o Each `then()` block returns a new promise, allowing you to chain multiple asynchronous operations in sequence.

Real-World Example: Making an API Call with Promises

Let's look at an example where we use a promise to make an **API call** to fetch data from a server. We'll use a **public API** to simulate an HTTP request.

Example: Fetching Data from a Public API

1. **HTML (index.html)**: Create a simple webpage with a button to trigger the API call and display the results.

```html
html
```

```html
<!DOCTYPE html>
```

```html
<html lang="en">
<head>
    <meta charset="UTF-8">
    <meta                     name="viewport"
content="width=device-width,        initial-
scale=1.0">
    <title>API Call with Promises</title>
</head>
<body>
    <h1>API Call Example</h1>
    <button  onclick="fetchUserData()">Get
User Data</button>
    <p id="userData"></p>


    <script src="script.js"></script>
</body>
</html>
```

2. **JavaScript (script.js)**: We will use the `fetch` API to retrieve data from a public API and display it on the webpage.

```javascript

function fetchUserData() {

fetch('https://jsonplaceholder.typicode.c
om/users/1') // Make API request
    .then(response => {
```

```
    if (!response.ok) {
        throw new Error("Network response
was not ok.");
    }
    return response.json(); // Parse the
JSON data
  })
  .then(data => {

document.getElementById('userData').inner
HTML   =   `Name:   ${data.name},   Email:
${data.email}`;
  })
  .catch(error => {

document.getElementById('userData').inner
HTML = `Error: ${error.message}`;
  });
}
```

How it works:

- We use the `fetch()` method to make an API call to a public API (`jsonplaceholder.typicode.com`).

- The `fetch()` method returns a promise. When the promise is resolved, the `then()` block is executed.

- Inside `then()`, we check if the response is successful (status code 200), and then parse the response data using `.json()`.

- The data is then displayed in the HTML element with the ID userData.
- If there's an error (e.g., network issues), it is caught by the catch() block, and an error message is displayed.

Summary

In this chapter, we learned how asynchronous programming works in JavaScript, and how to use **callbacks** and **promises** to handle asynchronous tasks. Callbacks provide a way to handle the results of an asynchronous operation, but they can lead to callback hell if overused. Promises make managing asynchronous operations more structured, allowing for cleaner code and better error handling. We also explored a real-world example of making an **API call** using promises, which is a common scenario in modern web applications. Understanding how to manage asynchronous operations is essential for building responsive, efficient applications in JavaScript.

CHAPTER 11

UNDERSTANDING ERROR HANDLING

Error handling is an essential part of writing robust and user-friendly JavaScript code. In this chapter, we will explore how to handle errors using `try`, `catch`, and `finally` statements, how to throw custom errors, and demonstrate a real-world example of handling errors in a form validation system.

Try, Catch, and Finally Statements

1. **The `try` Statement**:

    o   The `try` statement is used to wrap a block of code that might throw an error. JavaScript will attempt to execute the code inside the `try` block.

```javascript
javascript

try {
  let result = riskyFunction();
  console.log(result); // If riskyFunction
throws an error, the following line won't
run
}
```

- o   If no error occurs, the code inside the `try` block will execute as normal.

2. **The `catch` Statement**:

- o   The `catch` statement is used to handle errors that occur in the `try` block. If an error is thrown, the code inside the `catch` block will be executed.

javascript

```
try {
  let result = riskyFunction();
} catch (error) {
  console.log("An   error   occurred:   "   +
error.message);
}
```

- o   The `catch` block receives the error object as a parameter, which contains details about the error, such as its message and type.

3. **The `finally` Statement**:

- o   The `finally` statement is optional and can be used to execute code that should run **whether an error occurs or not**. It is useful for cleaning up resources or performing final operations after a `try` block, regardless of whether an error was caught.

javascript

```
try {
  let result = riskyFunction();
  console.log(result);
} catch (error) {
  console.log("An    error    occurred:    "    +
error.message);
} finally {
  console.log("This will always run.");
}
```

- o In this example, "This will always run." will be printed no matter what happens inside the `try` block.

4. **Error Propagation**:
   - o If an error is caught inside a `catch` block, it can be re-thrown to propagate it further if necessary. This is useful when you want to handle errors at a higher level in the call stack.

```
javascript
```

```
try {
  throw    new    Error("Something    went
wrong!");
} catch (error) {
  console.log(error.message);
  throw error; // Re-throwing the error
}
```

Throwing Custom Errors

In JavaScript, you can throw custom errors using the `throw` statement. This is useful when you want to enforce specific conditions or handle user-defined errors in your application.

1. **Throwing an Error**:
   o You can throw an error explicitly in your code when a condition fails. The `throw` statement is followed by an instance of the `Error` object or any other object that you want to throw.

```javascript
function checkAge(age) {
  if (age < 18) {
    throw new Error("You must be at least 18 years old.");
  }
  return "You are old enough!";
}

try {
  console.log(checkAge(16)); // Will throw an error
} catch (error) {
  console.log("Error: " + error.message);
  // Handling the error
}
```

o In this example, if the `age` is less than 18, the `checkAge` function throws a custom error, which is caught and logged by the `catch` block.

2. **Custom Error Types**:

o You can create custom error types by extending the built-in `Error` object. This allows you to provide more specific error handling for different scenarios.

```javascript
class AgeError extends Error {
  constructor(message) {
    super(message);  // Call the parent constructor
    this.name = "AgeError"; // Custom error name
  }
}

function checkAge(age) {
  if (age < 18) {
    throw new AgeError("You must be at least 18 years old.");
  }
  return "You are old enough!";
}

try {
```

```
    console.log(checkAge(16)); // Will throw
an AgeError
} catch (error) {
    console.log(`${error.name}:
${error.message}`); // Outputs: AgeError:
You must be at least 18 years old.
}
```

- o In this example, the custom `AgeError` class extends the `Error` object, providing a custom error type that can be used in your application.

Real-World Example: Handling Errors in a Form Validation System

Now let's apply error handling to a real-world scenario: **form validation**. When users fill out a form, we can use `try`, `catch`, and `finally` to handle errors like missing or invalid inputs.

Example: Form Validation with Error Handling

1. **HTML (index.html)**: Create a form with input fields for name, age, and email.

```
html
```

```
<!DOCTYPE html>
<html lang="en">
<head>
    <meta charset="UTF-8">
```

106

```
    <meta                    name="viewport"
content="width=device-width,        initial-
scale=1.0">
    <title>Form Validation</title>
</head>
<body>
    <h1>Registration Form</h1>
    <form id="registrationForm">
        <label for="name">Name:</label>
        <input     type="text"     id="name"
required><br><br>
        <label for="age">Age:</label>
        <input     type="number"    id="age"
required><br><br>
        <label for="email">Email:</label>
        <input    type="email"    id="email"
required><br><br>
        <button
type="submit">Submit</button>
    </form>
    <p id="error"></p>
    <script src="script.js"></script>
</body>
</html>
```

2. **JavaScript (script.js)**: Implement form validation that catches errors like empty fields or invalid age.

```javascript
javascript
```

```
document.getElementById("registrationForm
").addEventListener("submit",
function(event) {
  event.preventDefault();  // Prevent the
form from submitting until validation is
complete

  let           name           =
document.getElementById("name").value;
  let           age            =
document.getElementById("age").value;
  let           email          =
document.getElementById("email").value;
  let           errorMessage   =
document.getElementById("error");

  try {
    // Check for empty fields
    if (!name || !age || !email) {
      throw new Error("All fields are
required.");
    }

    // Validate age
    if (age < 18) {
      throw new Error("You must be at least
18 years old.");
    }
```

```javascript
    // Validate email format
    const emailPattern = /^[a-zA-Z0-9._-
]+@[a-zA-Z0-9.-]+\.[a-zA-Z]{2,6}$/;
    if (!emailPattern.test(email)) {
      throw new Error("Invalid email
address.");
    }

    // If everything is valid, show success
message
    errorMessage.textContent = "Form
submitted successfully!";
    errorMessage.style.color = "green";

  } catch (error) {
    // Catch and display error messages
    errorMessage.textContent = "Error: " +
error.message;
    errorMessage.style.color = "red";
  } finally {
    // This block runs regardless of
whether an error occurred or not
    console.log("Validation check
complete.");
  }
});
```

How it works:

- When the user submits the form, the `submit` event is caught, and the form validation logic is executed.
- We check if the fields are empty, if the age is valid (18 or older), and if the email matches a valid format.
- If any of these conditions fail, an error is thrown using the `throw` statement.
- The `catch` block catches the error and displays the message to the user.
- The `finally` block ensures that a message indicating that the validation check has completed is logged, regardless of the outcome.

Summary

In this chapter, we learned how to handle errors in JavaScript using `try`, `catch`, and `finally` statements. These statements help you manage errors gracefully, making your code more resilient and user-friendly. We also explored how to throw custom errors and how to handle errors in practical situations like form validation. By using error handling, you can ensure that your applications run smoothly, even when unexpected issues arise, and provide meaningful feedback to users when something goes wrong.

CHAPTER 12

WORKING WITH THE DOM (DOCUMENT OBJECT MODEL)

The **Document Object Model (DOM)** is an essential concept in JavaScript and web development. It provides a structured representation of an HTML document as a tree of objects. This chapter will introduce you to DOM manipulation, explain how to select, modify, and delete elements, and provide a real-world example of building a dynamic to-do list.

Introduction to DOM Manipulation

The **DOM** allows JavaScript to interact with HTML and CSS. Through the DOM, JavaScript can access and modify elements on the webpage, change their styles, add or remove content, and handle user interactions such as clicks and typing. In essence, the DOM is the bridge between the static HTML document and dynamic, interactive web pages.

JavaScript can manipulate the DOM using various methods that allow you to:

- **Access elements** (e.g., by their id, class, or tag name).
- **Modify element properties** (e.g., text, attributes, styles).

111

- **Delete elements** or add new elements dynamically.

Here are the basic concepts of DOM manipulation:

1. **Accessing the DOM**: You can select elements from the document using various DOM methods like `getElementById()`, `getElementsByClassName()`, `querySelector()`, etc.
2. **Modifying the DOM**: After selecting an element, you can modify its content, styles, or attributes.
3. **Creating and Deleting Elements**: You can create new elements with `createElement()` and append them to the document. You can also remove elements with `removeChild()` or `remove()`.

Selecting, Modifying, and Deleting Elements

1. **Selecting Elements**:
   - **`getElementById()`**: Selects an element by its unique `id` attribute.

     javascript

     ```
     let header = document.getElementById('header');
     ```

- o **getElementsByClassName()**: Selects all elements with a given class name (returns a live HTMLCollection).

  ```javascript
  let items = document.getElementsByClassName('item');
  ```

- o **querySelector()**: Selects the first element that matches a CSS selector.

  ```javascript
  let firstItem = document.querySelector('.item');
  ```

- o **querySelectorAll()**: Selects all elements that match a CSS selector (returns a static NodeList).

  ```javascript
  let allItems = document.querySelectorAll('.item');
  ```

2. **Modifying Elements**:

After selecting an element, you can modify its properties:

- o **Text Content**: Use `textContent` to change the text inside an element.

  javascript

  ```
  let         header         =
  document.getElementById('header');
  header.textContent  =  "New  Header
  Text";
  ```

- o **HTML Content**: Use `innerHTML` to change the HTML content inside an element.

  javascript

  ```
  let         list         =
  document.getElementById('list');
  list.innerHTML   =   "<li>New   List
  Item</li>"; // Replace all items
  ```

- o **Attributes**: Use `setAttribute()` to change an element's attribute (like `href`, `src`, `class`, etc.).

  javascript

  ```
  let         link         =
  document.getElementById('link');
  ```

114

```
link.setAttribute('href',
'https://www.example.com');
```

o **Styles**: Use the `style` property to modify inline styles.

```
javascript
```

```
let               button             =
document.getElementById('button');
button.style.backgroundColor      =
'blue';
button.style.color = 'white';
```

3. **Deleting Elements**:

You can remove elements from the DOM using `remove()` or `removeChild()`:

o **remove()**: Removes the element directly.

```
javascript
```

```
let                item               =
document.getElementById('item');
item.remove();   //   Removes   the
element from the DOM
```

o **removeChild()**: Removes a child element from a parent element.

115

```
javascript
```

```
let             list             =
document.getElementById('list');
let             item             =
document.getElementById('item');
list.removeChild(item);  // Removes
item from list
```

Real-World Example: Building a Dynamic To-Do List

Now that we have a basic understanding of DOM manipulation, let's build a **dynamic to-do list**. This list will allow users to add tasks, mark them as completed, and delete them.

1. **HTML (index.html)**:

```
html
```

```
<!DOCTYPE html>
<html lang="en">
<head>
    <meta charset="UTF-8">
    <meta              name="viewport"
content="width=device-width,     initial-
scale=1.0">
    <title>To-Do List</title>
</head>
<body>
    <h1>My To-Do List</h1>
```

116

```
    <input      type="text"      id="newTask"
placeholder="Add a new task">
    <button          onclick="addTask()">Add
Task</button>
    <ul id="taskList"></ul>


    <script src="script.js"></script>
</body>
</html>
```

2. **JavaScript (script.js)**:

Now, let's write the JavaScript code that allows users to add, complete, and delete tasks.

javascript

```
function addTask() {
  // Get the task input and create a new
list item
  let           taskInput           =
document.getElementById('newTask');
  let taskText = taskInput.value;

  if (taskText === "") {
    alert("Please enter a task!");
    return; // Don't add an empty task
  }

  // Create a new list item
```

117

```javascript
let li = document.createElement('li');
li.textContent = taskText;

// Add a button to mark the task as
completed
let            completeButton            =
document.createElement('button');
completeButton.textContent = "Complete";
completeButton.onclick = function() {
   li.style.textDecoration    =    "line-
through"; // Strikethrough the task text
   };

// Add a delete button to remove the task
let            deleteButton            =
document.createElement('button');
deleteButton.textContent = "Delete";
deleteButton.onclick = function() {
   li.remove(); // Remove the task from
the list
   };

// Append the buttons to the list item
li.appendChild(completeButton);
li.appendChild(deleteButton);

// Add the new task to the task list
```

```
document.getElementById('taskList').appen
dChild(li);

  // Clear the input field
  taskInput.value = "";
}
```

How it works:

- The addTask() function retrieves the value from the input field, creates a new <li> element for the task, and appends it to the task list (<ul>).
- For each task, two buttons are created: one to mark the task as complete (by striking through the text) and another to delete the task from the list.
- When the "Complete" button is clicked, the task text gets a line-through style, indicating that the task is done.
- When the "Delete" button is clicked, the task is removed from the DOM.

Summary

In this chapter, we explored how to interact with the DOM using JavaScript. We learned how to select, modify, and delete elements dynamically. The real-world example of building a dynamic to-do list demonstrated how DOM manipulation can be used to create interactive, user-driven web applications. By understanding DOM manipulation, you can add interactivity to your web pages, making them more dynamic and engaging for users.

CHAPTER 13

JAVASCRIPT ES6 AND BEYOND

ECMAScript 6 (ES6), also known as **ECMAScript 2015**, introduced a range of new features and syntax improvements to JavaScript, making the language more powerful, concise, and easier to work with. This chapter will cover some of the key ES6 features such as `let`, `const`, arrow functions, template literals, and new methods for objects and arrays. We will also provide a real-world example of refactoring older JavaScript code using these ES6 features.

Introduction to ES6 Features

1. **`let` and `const`**:
    o   Before ES6, JavaScript used the `var` keyword to declare variables. However, `var` has some scoping issues that led to unexpected behavior, especially in loops and functions.
    o   **`let`** and **`const`** were introduced to improve scoping and prevent common issues related to variable declarations.
    o   **`let`**: Used to declare variables with block scope. Variables declared with `let` can be reassigned.

121

```
javascript
```

```
let name = "Alice";
name = "Bob"; // Reassigned value is
allowed
```

- o **const**: Used to declare constants (variables that cannot be reassigned). Like let, const also has block scope.

```
javascript
```

```
const pi = 3.14159;
// pi = 3.14; // Error: Assignment to
constant variable
```

2. **Arrow Functions**:
   - o Arrow functions provide a more concise syntax for writing functions. They are also lexically scoped, meaning this inside an arrow function retains the value of this from the surrounding context.
   - o Traditional function syntax:

```
javascript
```

```
function greet(name) {
  return "Hello, " + name;
}
```

122

o Arrow function syntax:

javascript

```
const greet = (name) => {
  return "Hello, " + name;
};
```

o If the function body is a single expression, you can omit the braces and the `return` keyword:

javascript

```
const greet = (name) => "Hello, " +
name;
```

3. **Template Literals**:

o Template literals allow you to embed expressions inside strings using $ { } syntax, and they can span multiple lines.

javascript

```
let name = "Alice";
let greeting = `Hello, ${name}!`; // String
interpolation
console.log(greeting); // Outputs: "Hello,
Alice!"
```

o You can also create multi-line strings with template literals:

```javascript

let message = `This is a
multi-line
string.`;
console.log(message);
```

New Object and Array Methods

ES6 introduced several new methods for objects and arrays, making them easier to work with.

1. **Object Methods**:
   o **Object.assign()**: Copies the values of all enumerable properties from one or more source objects to a target object.

   ```javascript

   let target = { name: "Alice" };
   let source = { age: 25 };
   let result = Object.assign(target, source);
   console.log(result); // { name: "Alice", age: 25 }
   ```

- o **Object.keys()**: Returns an array of a given object's property names.

```javascript
let person = { name: "Alice", age: 25 };
let keys = Object.keys(person);
console.log(keys);    //    ["name", "age"]
```

- o **Object.values()**: Returns an array of a given object's property values.

```javascript
let person = { name: "Alice", age: 25 };
let values = Object.values(person);
console.log(values);   //   ["Alice", 25]
```

2. **Array Methods**:

- o **Array.from()**: Creates a new array from an array-like or iterable object.

```javascript
let str = "Hello";
```

```
let arr = Array.from(str);
console.log(arr); // ["H", "e", "l",
"l", "o"]
```

o **Array.find()**: Returns the first element in an array that satisfies the provided testing function.

javascript

```
let numbers = [1, 2, 3, 4, 5];
let found = numbers.find(num => num
> 3);
console.log(found); // 4
```

o **Array.includes()**: Checks if an array contains a specific element.

javascript

```
let fruits = ["apple", "banana",
"cherry"];
console.log(fruits.includes("banana
")); // true
console.log(fruits.includes("orange
")); // false
```

Real-World Example: Refactoring Code with ES6 Features

Let's take an older piece of JavaScript code and refactor it using ES6 features such as `let`, `const`, arrow functions, and template literals to improve readability and functionality.

Old JavaScript Code:

javascript

```javascript
var person = {
  firstName: "John",
  lastName: "Doe",
  age: 30,
  fullName: function() {
    return this.firstName + " " + this.lastName;
  },
  greet: function() {
    alert("Hello, " + this.fullName() + "!");
  }
};

person.greet();
```

Refactored ES6 Code:

javascript

```javascript
const person = {
  firstName: "John",
```

127

```
lastName: "Doe",
age: 30,

// Using ES6 shorthand method definition
fullName() {
    return `${this.firstName} ${this.lastName}`;
// Template literals
},

greet() {
    console.log(`Hello,    ${this.fullName()}!`);
// Template literals and console.log instead of
alert
    }
};

person.greet();
```

Changes Made:

1. **const**: The `person` object is declared using `const` since it doesn't need to be reassigned.

2. **Arrow Functions**: The method `fullName()` is written using ES6 shorthand syntax.

3. **Template Literals**: The `fullName()` method and the `greet()` method use template literals to concatenate strings, improving readability.

4. **Console Output**: Replaced `alert()` with `console.log()` for better development experience.

Summary

In this chapter, we explored the features introduced in **ES6** and beyond, which significantly improved the readability and maintainability of JavaScript code. We discussed how **let** and **const** improve variable scoping, how **arrow functions** provide cleaner syntax and fix issues with the `this` keyword, and how **template literals** make string manipulation easier. Additionally, we explored new methods for working with objects and arrays, such as **Object.assign()**, **Object.keys()**, **Array.find()**, and **Array.includes()**.

Finally, we demonstrated how to refactor older JavaScript code by incorporating ES6 features, which resulted in cleaner, more modern code. Understanding and using ES6 features is essential for writing efficient, maintainable JavaScript.

CHAPTER 14

JAVASCRIPT CLASSES AND OOP (OBJECT-ORIENTED PROGRAMMING)

Object-Oriented Programming (OOP) is a programming paradigm that is based on the concept of **objects**, which are instances of **classes**. In JavaScript, OOP allows you to model real-world entities and their interactions. This chapter will introduce the principles of OOP in JavaScript, explain how to create and use classes and objects, and provide a real-world example of building a class-based **e-commerce cart**.

Introduction to OOP Principles in JavaScript

1. **What is OOP?**

   o Object-Oriented Programming (OOP) is a programming style that organizes software design around data, or objects, rather than functions and logic. The primary principles of OOP include:

     ▪ **Encapsulation**: Wrapping data and methods that operate on that data into a single unit (class). This helps to protect the data by limiting direct access to it.

- **Abstraction**: Hiding complex implementation details and exposing only the necessary parts of an object or class.
- **Inheritance**: Allows one class to inherit properties and methods from another class, promoting code reusability.
- **Polymorphism**: Enables objects of different classes to be treated as objects of a common superclass, making it easier to extend and modify code.

2. **Why Use OOP in JavaScript?**

   o OOP is widely used in JavaScript to create scalable, maintainable, and modular code. By organizing your code into objects and classes, you can model real-world behaviors and relationships, making your code more intuitive and easier to manage.

Creating and Using Classes and Objects

1. **Creating Classes**:

   o A class in JavaScript is a blueprint for creating objects with shared properties and methods.

Classes are defined using the `class` keyword followed by the class name.

```javascript

class Car {
  // Constructor method to initialize object properties
  constructor(make, model, year) {
    this.make = make;
    this.model = model;
    this.year = year;
  }

  // Method to display car details
  displayDetails() {
    console.log(`${this.year} ${this.make} ${this.model}`);
  }
}
```

In this example, the `Car` class has a constructor to initialize the `make`, `model`, and `year` properties, and a method `displayDetails()` to show the car's information.

2. **Creating Objects**:

   o Once a class is defined, you can create instances (objects) of that class by using the `new` keyword.

132

javascript

```
let myCar = new Car("Toyota", "Camry", 2021);
myCar.displayDetails(); // Outputs: "2021 Toyota Camry"
```

3. **Constructor Method**:

   o The `constructor()` method is a special method for initializing new objects. It runs automatically when a new instance of the class is created.

javascript

```
class Person {
  constructor(name, age) {
    this.name = name;
    this.age = age;
  }
}
let person1 = new Person("Alice", 30);
```

4. **Methods in Classes**:

   o Classes can have methods that perform actions on the object's data. These methods are defined inside the class body.

javascript

```
class Rectangle {
  constructor(width, height) {
    this.width = width;
    this.height = height;
  }

  // Method to calculate the area of the
rectangle
  calculateArea() {
    return this.width * this.height;
  }
}

let rect = new Rectangle(5, 10);
console.log(rect.calculateArea());       //
Outputs: 50
```

Real-World Example: Building a Class-Based E-Commerce Cart

In this example, we'll create a simple **e-commerce cart** using JavaScript classes and OOP principles. The cart will allow users to add items, remove items, and calculate the total price.

1. **HTML (index.html)**: Create a basic HTML structure to interact with the cart.

```
html
```

```
<!DOCTYPE html>
```

```
<html lang="en">
<head>
    <meta charset="UTF-8">
    <meta                     name="viewport"
content="width=device-width,        initial-
scale=1.0">
    <title>E-Commerce Cart</title>
</head>
<body>
    <h1>Shopping Cart</h1>
    <button     onclick="addToCart('Apple',
1.5)">Add Apple ($1.5)</button>
    <button    onclick="addToCart('Banana',
1.0)">Add Banana ($1.0)</button>
    <button
onclick="removeFromCart('Apple')">Remove
Apple</button>
    <h2>Your Cart</h2>
    <ul id="cartItems"></ul>
    <p id="totalPrice">Total: $0</p>
    <script src="script.js"></script>
</body>
</html>
```

2. **JavaScript (script.js)**: Now let's create the `Cart` class and implement methods to add items, remove items, and calculate the total price.

```
javascript
```

```javascript
class Cart {
  constructor() {
    this.items = []; // Array to store cart items
  }

  // Method to add an item to the cart
  addItem(item, price) {
    this.items.push({ item, price });
  }

  // Method to remove an item from the cart
  removeItem(item) {
    this.items                            =
this.items.filter(cartItem              =>
cartItem.item !== item);
  }

  // Method to calculate the total price of
the cart
  calculateTotal() {
    return        this.items.reduce((total,
cartItem) => total + cartItem.price, 0);
  }

  // Method to display the items in the
cart
  displayItems() {
```

```javascript
    let           cartList           =
document.getElementById('cartItems');
    cartList.innerHTML = "";  // Clear
previous list
    this.items.forEach(cartItem => {
      let             li              =
document.createElement('li');
      li.textContent = `${cartItem.item} -
$${cartItem.price}`;
      cartList.appendChild(li);
    });
  }


  // Method to display the total price
  displayTotal() {
    let total = this.calculateTotal();

document.getElementById('totalPrice').tex
tContent = `Total: $${total.toFixed(2)}`;
  }
}


// Create a new Cart instance
let myCart = new Cart();


// Add item to the cart
function addToCart(item, price) {
  myCart.addItem(item, price);
  myCart.displayItems();
```

```
    myCart.displayTotal();
}

// Remove item from the cart
function removeFromCart(item) {
  myCart.removeItem(item);
  myCart.displayItems();
  myCart.displayTotal();
}
```

How it works:

- The `Cart` class has a constructor that initializes an empty `items` array.
- The `addItem()` method allows you to add items to the cart, and the `removeItem()` method removes items.
- The `calculateTotal()` method sums up the prices of the items in the cart.
- The `displayItems()` and `displayTotal()` methods are used to update the user interface with the current list of items and the total price.
- The `addToCart()` and `removeFromCart()` functions are used to interact with the cart when the user clicks the corresponding buttons.

Summary

In this chapter, we learned the principles of **Object-Oriented Programming (OOP)** in JavaScript. We discussed the key concepts of **encapsulation**, **abstraction**, **inheritance**, and **polymorphism**. We also explored how to create and use **classes** and **objects**, and how these concepts help organize and manage code in a more modular and scalable way.

Using a real-world example, we built a **class-based e-commerce cart** that allows users to add, remove, and view items while calculating the total price. By using OOP principles and JavaScript classes, we can build complex systems that are easier to maintain, extend, and modify in the future.

CHAPTER 15

WORKING WITH MODULES

In JavaScript, especially with the advent of **ES6** (ECMAScript 2015), modules became a powerful way to organize code into reusable, manageable pieces. In this chapter, we will explore the concept of **ES6 modules**, the `export` and `import` syntax, and demonstrate how to organize large projects using modules. We'll also provide a real-world example of splitting a large project into smaller, more manageable modules.

Understanding ES6 Modules: Export and Import

Modules in JavaScript allow you to divide your code into separate files, each containing specific functionality. The idea is to write modular, reusable code that can be shared across different parts of an application.

1. **Exporting a Module**:
    o To make code available to other files, we use the `export` keyword. You can export functions, objects, or variables from a module so that they can be imported and used in other files.

    Named Exports: You can export multiple items from a module.

140

```
javascript
```

```javascript
// math.js (module)
export const add = (a, b) => a + b;
export const subtract = (a, b) => a - b;
```

Default Export: You can export a single item as the default export from a module.

```
javascript
```

```javascript
// logger.js (module)
const logMessage = (message) => {
  console.log(message);
};
export default logMessage;
```

- o Here, the `add` and `subtract` functions are exported with **named exports**, while `logMessage` is exported as a **default export**.

2. **Importing a Module**:
   - o To use the exported items from another module, we use the `import` keyword.

Importing Named Exports:

```
javascript
```

```javascript
// main.js
```

```
import { add, subtract } from './math.js';
console.log(add(2, 3)); // Outputs: 5
console.log(subtract(5, 3)); // Outputs: 2
```

Importing Default Exports:

```
javascript
```

```
// main.js
import logMessage from './logger.js';
logMessage("Hello, world!"); // Outputs:
Hello, world!
```

- o When using named exports, you import each item by its exact name. For default exports, you can choose any name for the imported module (in this case, we used logMessage).

3. **Importing All Exports from a Module**:
   - o If you want to import all exports from a module as a single object, you can use the * as syntax.

```
javascript
```

```
// main.js
import * as math from './math.js';
console.log(math.add(2, 3)); // Outputs: 5
console.log(math.subtract(5,    3));    //
Outputs: 2
```

o This imports everything from the `math.js` module and makes it available as the `math` object.

Organizing Code with Modules

Modules provide a way to organize your code into logical units. By breaking large projects into smaller, manageable modules, you make your code easier to maintain, test, and extend.

1. **Creating a Modular Project**:
   o Divide the functionality of your application into different files (modules). Each module should focus on a specific concern, such as user authentication, handling API requests, or performing utility functions.

2. **Benefits of Using Modules**:
   o **Reusability**: Once you write a module, you can reuse it across different parts of your application or even in different projects.
   o **Maintainability**: With separate files for different features, it's easier to find and modify code without affecting other parts of the application.
   o **Encapsulation**: Modules allow you to encapsulate functionality and expose only what's necessary, preventing global namespace pollution.

3. **Directory Structure**:

- o When organizing your project, it's a good practice to create a directory structure that clearly separates concerns.

Example directory structure:

```bash
/src
  /utils
    math.js
    logger.js
  /app
    user.js
    api.js
  index.js
```

- o In this example, utility functions (math.js, logger.js) are in the /utils folder, while application-related files (user.js, api.js) are in the /app folder.

Real-World Example: Splitting a Large Project into Manageable Modules

Let's take a simple project that involves managing user data and making API requests. We'll refactor this project to use **modules**, making it easier to maintain and extend.

1. **Creating Modules for the Project**:

   o **API Module** (handles API requests):

   javascript

   ```javascript
   // src/utils/api.js
   export const fetchUserData = async
   (userId) => {
     try {
       const response = await
   fetch(`https://jsonplaceholder.typi
   code.com/users/${userId}`);
       const data = await
   response.json();
       return data;
     } catch (error) {
       console.error("Error   fetching
   user data:", error);
     }
   };
   ```

   o **User Module** (handles user data processing):

   javascript

   ```javascript
   // src/app/user.js
   import { fetchUserData } from
   '../utils/api.js';
   ```

145

```javascript
export const getUser = async (userId)
=> {
  const      userData      =      await
fetchUserData(userId);
    console.log("User          Data:",
userData);
};
```

- o **Logger Module** (handles logging):

```
javascript
```

```javascript
// src/utils/logger.js
const logMessage = (message) => {
    console.log(message);
};
```

```javascript
export default logMessage;
```

2. **Using the Modules in the Main Application**:

```
javascript
```

```javascript
// src/index.js
import            logMessage            from
'./utils/logger.js';
import { getUser } from './app/user.js';
```

```javascript
logMessage("Starting the application...");
```

146

```
// Fetch and display user data
getUser(1);
```

- o In the `src/index.js` file, we import the necessary functions from the modules:
  - `logMessage` from `logger.js` to log messages.
  - `getUser` from `user.js` to fetch and display user data.

3. **Directory Structure**: After refactoring, your project's directory structure might look like this:

```bash
/src
  /utils
    api.js
    logger.js
  /app
    user.js
  index.js
```

4. **Benefits**:
   - o **Reusability**: The `api.js` module can be reused for any API-related tasks across different parts of the application.
   - o **Maintainability**: If the API changes, you only need to modify the `api.js` module, and all other

147

parts of the app that rely on it will automatically benefit from the update.

o **Separation of Concerns**: Each module handles a specific part of the application (e.g., fetching user data, logging messages), making the code more organized and easier to test.

Summary

In this chapter, we learned how to work with **ES6 modules** in JavaScript to break down large projects into smaller, manageable pieces. We explored how to use the `export` and `import` keywords to share functionality between files, and how to organize code using modules to improve **maintainability**, **reusability**, and **separation of concerns**. Using a real-world example, we refactored a project into multiple modules that each handle a specific task, making the code more modular and easier to extend. Understanding modules is crucial for working on larger applications and modern JavaScript development.

CHAPTER 16

JAVASCRIPT DESIGN PATTERNS

Design patterns are standard solutions to common problems in software design. These patterns are reusable, proven solutions to specific types of issues that arise in programming. In JavaScript, design patterns help to organize and manage code, making it more maintainable, scalable, and easier to understand. In this chapter, we will explore some common design patterns—**Singleton**, **Factory**, and **Module**—discuss their benefits, and provide a real-world example of using the **Singleton pattern** for a data manager.

Introduction to Common Design Patterns

1. **Singleton Pattern**:
    - The **Singleton** pattern ensures that a class has only **one instance** and provides a global point of access to that instance. This pattern is particularly useful when you need to manage shared resources, such as a database connection or a configuration manager, across an application.

    Key Characteristics:

    - One instance of the class.
    - Global access to that instance.

149

o Lazy instantiation (only created when needed).

Example use cases: Configuration settings, logging systems, database connections.

2. **Factory Pattern**:
   o The **Factory** pattern provides a way to create objects without specifying the exact class of object that will be created. It abstracts the instantiation process, making it more flexible and decoupling object creation from its usage.

   Key Characteristics:

   o An interface for creating objects.
   o Objects are created dynamically, based on the parameters passed.

Example use cases: Object creation in applications that require different types of products or services.

3. **Module Pattern**:
   o The **Module** pattern is used to create a self-contained unit of functionality that exposes a public API while keeping internal details private. This pattern is widely used for organizing code in JavaScript, especially in larger applications, to avoid polluting the global scope.

Key Characteristics:

- o Encapsulation of data and functionality.
- o Public API that interacts with private internal state.
- o Avoids global scope pollution.

Example use cases: Creating utility libraries, managing application state.

Benefits of Using Design Patterns in JavaScript

1. **Code Reusability**:
   - o Design patterns help to solve common problems in a standardized way. Once a pattern is understood and implemented, it can be reused in different parts of an application or across multiple projects.

2. **Maintainability**:
   - o Design patterns lead to cleaner and more organized code. They allow for easier updates and maintenance because common solutions are applied consistently across the codebase.

3. **Scalability**:
   - o Design patterns help to structure code in a way that makes it easier to scale. As projects grow in size and complexity, using design patterns

151

ensures that the code remains modular, maintainable, and adaptable to change.

4. **Easier Debugging**:

   o Because design patterns are based on proven solutions, they reduce the likelihood of bugs and errors, making it easier to identify and fix issues when they arise.

5. **Communication**:

   o Using design patterns improves communication among developers. Since design patterns are widely recognized and understood, they provide a common vocabulary for describing solutions.

Real-World Example: Implementing a Singleton Pattern for a Data Manager

Let's implement the **Singleton pattern** to manage a **data manager** that ensures only one instance of the data manager exists in the application. This data manager will handle operations like fetching data and storing data, and we'll make sure that only a single instance of the data manager can be created.

1. **Singleton Pattern for Data Manager**

   The following code demonstrates the Singleton pattern to manage a single instance of a `DataManager` class.

   ```
   javascript
   ```

152

```javascript
class DataManager {
  // Step 1: Create a private static
  variable to hold the instance
  static instance = null;

  // Step 2: Constructor to initialize the
  data manager
  constructor() {
    if (DataManager.instance) {
      // If an instance already exists,
      return the existing instance
      return DataManager.instance;
    }

    // Initialize instance properties
    this.data = [];

    // Step 3: Save the instance to the
    static variable
    DataManager.instance = this;
  }

  // Method to add data to the manager
  addData(item) {
    this.data.push(item);
  }
```

```
  // Method to get all data from the
manager
  getData() {
    return this.data;
  }

  // Method to clear all data in the
manager
  clearData() {
    this.data = [];
  }
}

// Step 4: Usage of the Singleton pattern
const dataManager1 = new DataManager();
dataManager1.addData("Item 1");
dataManager1.addData("Item 2");

const dataManager2 = new DataManager(); //
This should refer to the same instance as
dataManager1

console.log(dataManager1.getData());    //
["Item 1", "Item 2"]
console.log(dataManager2.getData());    //
["Item 1", "Item 2"]

// Clear data in dataManager2
dataManager2.clearData();
```

```
console.log(dataManager1.getData()); // []
(data is cleared in both instances)
console.log(dataManager2.getData()); // []
(same instance)
```

How it works:

- **Singleton Behavior**: The `DataManager` class uses a static `instance` property to ensure that only one instance of the class is ever created. The constructor checks whether an instance already exists, and if it does, it returns the existing instance instead of creating a new one.

- **Shared State**: Since both `dataManager1` and `dataManager2` are references to the same instance, any changes made to the data (e.g., clearing the data) will affect both references.

- **Global Access**: The `DataManager` ensures that throughout the application, the data manager remains consistent and centralized, which is useful for managing resources like application settings, global data, or server connections.

2. **Explanation of the Code**:

    o **Static Variable**: `static instance = null;` ensures that only one instance of the class is ever created. The `instance` variable is used to hold the unique instance of the `DataManager`.

- o **Constructor Logic**: The `constructor` checks if an instance of `DataManager` already exists. If it does, it returns the existing instance (`return DataManager.instance`). Otherwise, it creates a new instance and assigns it to the `instance` property.

- o **Data Management**: The methods `addData()`, `getData()`, and `clearData()` are used to manipulate and access the data in the `data` array. Since all methods refer to the same instance, any changes to the data affect all references to that instance.

3. **When to Use the Singleton Pattern**:

- o The **Singleton pattern** is useful in scenarios where you need to ensure that only one instance of a class exists, such as managing application-wide configurations, accessing a single database connection, or handling user sessions.

- o By using a Singleton, you can guarantee that only one instance controls access to the resource, avoiding issues like conflicting data or redundant operations.

156

Summary

In this chapter, we explored the concept of **JavaScript Design Patterns**, with a focus on the **Singleton pattern**. Design patterns provide proven solutions to common problems and help in organizing code to make it more maintainable, scalable, and reusable. We also covered other design patterns like the **Factory** and **Module** patterns, but we focused on implementing the **Singleton pattern** for managing a centralized data manager. By using the Singleton pattern, we ensure that only one instance of a class exists, allowing us to manage resources efficiently across an application. Understanding and applying design patterns is crucial for writing clean, modular, and efficient JavaScript code.

CHAPTER 17

JAVASCRIPT AND WEB APIS

Web APIs (Application Programming Interfaces) allow JavaScript to interact with external data and services, making it possible to fetch data from the internet, store information locally, or access hardware features such as geolocation. In this chapter, we will explore how to use JavaScript to interact with various Web APIs, including the **Fetch API**, **Geolocation API**, and **localStorage**. We will also build a real-world **weather app** that uses external API data to display weather information.

Introduction to Web APIs

Web APIs provide a way for JavaScript to interact with resources and services outside of the browser or application. These APIs expose certain functionalities to web applications, allowing developers to perform tasks like retrieving data, interacting with maps, saving data in the browser, or working with the user's device.

Some common Web APIs include:

1. **Fetch API**:
    o The `fetch()` function allows you to make **HTTP requests** to external servers to retrieve

data (such as JSON or HTML) or send data to the server. It's a modern replacement for `XMLHttpRequest`.

2. **Geolocation API**:
   o The `geolocation` API allows you to retrieve the geographical position of the user's device, enabling location-based services.

3. **localStorage API**:
   o The `localStorage` API allows you to store data locally in the user's browser, providing persistent storage that can be used across page reloads or sessions.

Using the Fetch API for HTTP Requests

The **Fetch API** allows you to make asynchronous HTTP requests to retrieve or send data to a server. It returns a **promise**, which allows you to handle the data once the request is completed.

1. **Basic Syntax of Fetch**:

```javascript
fetch(url)
    .then(response => response.json()) // Parse the response as JSON
    .then(data => console.log(data)) // Handle the data
```

```
.catch(error    =>    console.log('Error:',
error)); // Handle errors
```

- o url: The URL you want to request data from.
- o .then(response => response.json()): The response is parsed as JSON data.
- o .catch(error   => console.log('Error:', error)): Error handling if something goes wrong during the fetch request.

2. **Making GET Requests**:

- o The default method for fetch() is GET, which is used to request data from a server.

```javascript
fetch('https://jsonplaceholder.typicode.com/posts')
  .then(response => response.json())
  .then(data => console.log(data))
  .catch(error    =>    console.log('Error:',
error));
```

- o In this example, we make a GET request to the jsonplaceholder API and log the returned data.

3. **Making POST Requests**:

- o To send data to the server, you can specify the method as POST and include a body with the data.

```javascript
const postData = {
  title: 'foo',
  body: 'bar',
  userId: 1
};

fetch('https://jsonplaceholder.typicode.com/posts', {
  method: 'POST',
  headers: {
    'Content-Type': 'application/json'
  },
  body: JSON.stringify(postData) // Send data as a JSON string
})
  .then(response => response.json())
  .then(data => console.log(data))
  .catch(error => console.log('Error:', error));
```

- o This example demonstrates how to send a POST request with a JSON payload to the server.

Geolocation API

The **Geolocation API** allows JavaScript to get the geographical location of the user's device. This can be useful for building applications like maps, weather apps, or location-based services.

1. **Getting the User's Location**:
   o You can use `navigator.geolocation.getCurrentPosition()` to retrieve the current location of the user.

```javascript
if (navigator.geolocation) {

navigator.geolocation.getCurrentPosition(
    (position) => {
      console.log('Latitude:',
position.coords.latitude);
      console.log('Longitude:',
position.coords.longitude);
    },
    (error) => {
      console.log('Error getting
location:', error);
    }
  );
} else {
```

```
console.log('Geolocation      is       not
supported by this browser.');
}
```

- o This code checks if geolocation is supported in the browser. If so, it retrieves the user's latitude and longitude using `getCurrentPosition()`.
- o If an error occurs (e.g., the user denies location access), the `error` callback is called.

Using localStorage for Persistent Data Storage

The **localStorage** API provides a way to store data locally in the user's browser. Unlike cookies, the data stored in `localStorage` is persistent and doesn't expire when the browser is closed.

1. **Saving Data to localStorage**:
   - o Use `localStorage.setItem()` to store data.

   javascript

   ```
   localStorage.setItem('username', 'Alice');
   ```

2. **Retrieving Data from localStorage**:
   - o Use `localStorage.getItem()` to retrieve stored data.

   javascript

163

```
let                username                =
localStorage.getItem('username');
console.log(username); // Outputs: Alice
```

3. **Removing Data from localStorage**:

   o Use `localStorage.removeItem()` to remove an item.

   javascript

   ```
   localStorage.removeItem('username');
   ```

4. **Clearing All Data from localStorage**:

   o Use `localStorage.clear()` to remove all stored data.

   javascript

   ```
   localStorage.clear();
   ```

Real-World Example: Creating a Weather App with External API Data

Let's build a **weather app** that fetches weather data from a public API and displays it to the user. We will use the **Fetch API** to retrieve weather data, the **Geolocation API** to get the user's location, and `localStorage` to save the last fetched weather data.

164

1. **HTML (index.html)**: Set up the basic structure for the weather app.

html

```
<!DOCTYPE html>
<html lang="en">
<head>
  <meta charset="UTF-8">
  <meta                name="viewport"
content="width=device-width,       initial-
scale=1.0">
  <title>Weather App</title>
</head>
<body>
  <h1>Weather App</h1>
  <button        onclick="getWeather()">Get
Weather</button>
  <p id="weather">Weather data will appear
here.</p>
  <script src="script.js"></script>
</body>
</html>
```

2. **JavaScript (script.js)**: The script will use the **Geolocation API** to get the user's location and the **Fetch API** to retrieve the weather data.

javascript

```javascript
function getWeather() {
  if (navigator.geolocation) {

navigator.geolocation.getCurrentPosition(
fetchWeatherData, showError);
  } else {

document.getElementById('weather').innerT
ext = "Geolocation is not supported by this
browser.";
  }
}


function fetchWeatherData(position) {
  const lat = position.coords.latitude;
  const lon = position.coords.longitude;
  const apiKey = 'your-api-key'; // Replace
with your OpenWeatherMap API key
  const                   url                =
`https://api.openweathermap.org/data/2.5/
weather?lat=${lat}&lon=${lon}&appid=${api
Key}&units=metric`;

  fetch(url)
    .then(response => response.json())
    .then(data => {
      const       weatherDescription       =
data.weather[0].description;
```

```
      const temperature = data.main.temp;
      const city = data.name;
      const   weatherInfo   =   `Weather   in
${city}:              ${weatherDescription},
${temperature}°C`;


      // Display the weather data

document.getElementById('weather').innerT
ext = weatherInfo;


      // Save the data in localStorage
      localStorage.setItem('weather',
JSON.stringify(data));
    })
    .catch(error => {
      console.log('Error  fetching  weather
data:', error);

document.getElementById('weather').innerT
ext = "Failed to fetch weather data.";
    });
}


function showError(error) {
  switch(error.code) {
    case error.PERMISSION_DENIED:

document.getElementById('weather').innerT
```

```
ext = "User denied the request for
Geolocation.";
      break;
   case error.POSITION_UNAVAILABLE:

document.getElementById('weather').innerT
ext = "Location information is
unavailable.";
      break;
   case error.TIMEOUT:

document.getElementById('weather').innerT
ext = "The request to get user location
timed out.";
      break;
   case error.UNKNOWN_ERROR:

document.getElementById('weather').innerT
ext = "An unknown error occurred.";
      break;
  }
}
```

How it works:

- When the user clicks the "Get Weather" button, the app first checks if geolocation is available. If so, it fetches the user's location and calls the `fetchWeatherData` function to retrieve weather data from the OpenWeatherMap API.

- The weather data is displayed on the page, and the fetched data is stored in `localStorage` for later use.
- If the user denies the geolocation request or if there's an error, the `showError` function handles the error appropriately.

Summary

In this chapter, we explored several key **Web APIs** in JavaScript, including the **Fetch API**, **Geolocation API**, and **localStorage API**. We learned how to use the Fetch API to make HTTP requests, the Geolocation API to get the user's location, and how to store data in the browser using `localStorage`. Using these APIs, we built a **weather app** that retrieves and displays weather data based on the user's location, demonstrating how JavaScript can interact with external services to create dynamic and interactive web applications.

CHAPTER 18

WORKING WITH JSON (JAVASCRIPT OBJECT NOTATION)

In modern web development, **JSON (JavaScript Object Notation)** is one of the most widely used formats for exchanging data between a client and server. It is lightweight, easy to read, and easy to parse, making it ideal for storing and transmitting data. In this chapter, we'll explore what **JSON** is, how to **parse** and **stringify** data, and demonstrate a real-world example of storing user preferences in JSON format.

What is JSON and How to Parse and Stringify Data

1. **What is JSON?**
   - o **JSON** stands for **JavaScript Object Notation**. It is a text-based format that is used for representing structured data based on JavaScript object syntax. JSON is language-independent, meaning it can be used in any programming language, but it has its origins in JavaScript.
   - o JSON is commonly used to transmit data between a server and a client, especially in web APIs.

170

JSON data is made up of:

- o **Objects**: Key-value pairs enclosed in curly braces { }.
- o **Arrays**: Ordered lists of values enclosed in square brackets [].
- o **Values**: Strings, numbers, booleans, arrays, objects, or null.

Example of a JSON object:

json

```
{
  "name": "Alice",
  "age": 30,
  "isMember": true,
  "preferences": {
    "theme": "dark",
    "notifications": true
  }
}
```

2. **Parsing JSON Data**:
   - o **Parsing** is the process of converting a JSON string into a JavaScript object that can be used in your application.

o   To parse a JSON string, use the `JSON.parse()` method.

```javascript
const jsonString = '{"name": "Alice", "age": 30}';
const obj = JSON.parse(jsonString);
console.log(obj.name); // Outputs: Alice
console.log(obj.age);  // Outputs: 30
```

o   In this example, the `JSON.parse()` method converts the `jsonString` into a JavaScript object.

3. **Stringifying JavaScript Objects**:

   o   **Stringifying** is the process of converting a JavaScript object into a JSON string. This is useful when you need to send data to a server or save it locally.

   o   To stringify a JavaScript object, use the `JSON.stringify()` method.

```javascript
const obj = { name: "Alice", age: 30 };
const jsonString = JSON.stringify(obj);
console.log(jsonString);    // Outputs: '{"name":"Alice","age":30}'
```

o In this example, the `JSON.stringify()`
method converts the `obj` into a JSON string.

Real-World Example: Storing User Preferences in JSON Format

A common use case for JSON is storing and retrieving data, such as user preferences. Let's build a simple example where we store the user's theme choice and notification preferences in the browser's `localStorage` in JSON format.

1. **HTML (index.html)**: We will create a simple form that allows the user to select their theme and whether they want to receive notifications.

html

```
<!DOCTYPE html>
<html lang="en">
<head>
  <meta charset="UTF-8">
  <meta                       name="viewport"
content="width=device-width,        initial-
scale=1.0">
  <title>User Preferences</title>
</head>
<body>
  <h1>User Preferences</h1>
  <form id="preferencesForm">
    <label for="theme">Theme:</label>
```

173

```html
<select id="theme">
  <option value="light">Light</option>
  <option value="dark">Dark</option>
</select>
<br>
<label      for="notifications">Enable
Notifications:</label>
<input                 type="checkbox"
id="notifications">
<br><br>
<button              type="submit">Save
Preferences</button>
  </form>
  <p id="status"></p>

  <script src="script.js"></script>
</body>
</html>
```

2. **JavaScript (script.js)**: We will write JavaScript to save the user preferences in JSON format and retrieve them when the page loads.

```javascript
javascript


// Function  to  save  preferences  to
localStorage
function savePreferences(event) {
```

```javascript
    event.preventDefault(); // Prevent form
submission

    const                    theme                =
document.getElementById('theme').value;
    const           notifications              =
document.getElementById('notifications').
checked;

    const preferences = {
      theme: theme,
      notifications: notifications
    };

    // Convert the preferences object to a
JSON string
      localStorage.setItem('userPreferences',
JSON.stringify(preferences));

    // Show status message

document.getElementById('status').textCon
tent = 'Preferences saved!';
    }

// Function to load preferences from
localStorage
function loadPreferences() {
```

```javascript
const          preferences          =
localStorage.getItem('userPreferences');

  if (preferences) {
    // Parse the JSON string back into an
object
    const          parsedPreferences          =
JSON.parse(preferences);

    // Set form values based on stored
preferences

document.getElementById('theme').value   =
parsedPreferences.theme;

document.getElementById('notifications').
checked = parsedPreferences.notifications;
  }
}

// Event listener for form submission
document.getElementById('preferencesForm'
).addEventListener('submit',
savePreferences);

// Load preferences when the page loads
window.onload = loadPreferences;
```

How it works:

- **Saving Preferences**:
  - When the user submits the form, the `savePreferences` function is triggered. It retrieves the selected theme and notification preferences, then stores them in `localStorage` as a JSON string using `JSON.stringify()`.

- **Loading Preferences**:
  - When the page loads, the `loadPreferences` function checks if the user's preferences are stored in `localStorage`. If preferences exist, they are parsed using `JSON.parse()` and the form is populated with the saved values.

- **localStorage**:
  - `localStorage` is used to store the preferences so that they persist even after the user closes the browser or reloads the page. The data remains available across sessions until it is cleared by the user or through code.

Advantages of Using JSON for Storing Data

1. **Lightweight**:
   - JSON is a lightweight format for data exchange, which makes it ideal for storing simple data like user preferences or small datasets.

2. **Human-readable**:

177

- o JSON is easy to read and write for both humans and machines, making it a popular choice for configuration files, logging, and data transmission.

3. **Cross-platform Compatibility**:

- o JSON is supported in nearly every programming language and is the standard format for most web APIs. This makes it perfect for sharing data between different systems.

4. **Ease of Use with JavaScript**:

- o JavaScript natively supports JSON through `JSON.parse()` and `JSON.stringify()`, making it seamless to work with in the context of web applications.

Summary

In this chapter, we learned how to work with **JSON (JavaScript Object Notation)** in JavaScript, including how to **parse** JSON data from a string into a JavaScript object using `JSON.parse()` and how to **stringify** a JavaScript object into a JSON string using `JSON.stringify()`. We also explored a real-world example of **storing user preferences** in JSON format using `localStorage`. By using JSON, we can store and retrieve data efficiently in web applications, providing persistent storage and making data exchanges easy between the server and client. JSON is an essential tool in modern JavaScript development, especially when working with APIs and browser storage.

CHAPTER 19

TESTING AND DEBUGGING JAVASCRIPT

Testing and debugging are critical steps in ensuring that your JavaScript code works correctly and efficiently. In this chapter, we will cover the basics of debugging JavaScript code, introduce unit testing, and demonstrate how to write and run tests for a real-world scenario—a form submission function.

Introduction to Debugging Techniques and Tools

Debugging is the process of identifying and fixing errors in your code. JavaScript offers several techniques and tools to help you debug and troubleshoot issues efficiently.

1. **Console Logging**:
   o **console.log()** is one of the most basic and widely used debugging tools. You can use it to print out variables, check the flow of execution, and track errors.

```javascript
let num = 10;
```

180

```
console.log(num); // Outputs: 10
```

  o You can also log multiple values and objects to understand what's going wrong in your code.

```
javascript

let user = { name: "Alice", age: 30 };
console.log(user); // Outputs: { name:
"Alice", age: 30 }
```

2. **Breakpoints in Browser DevTools**:

  o Modern browsers like Chrome and Firefox come with built-in developer tools that allow you to set **breakpoints** in your code. A breakpoint pauses the execution of your code at a specific line, allowing you to inspect variables, the call stack, and the execution flow at that point in time.

  o To set a breakpoint:

    ▪ Open the **DevTools** (usually by pressing F12 or Ctrl+Shift+I).

    ▪ Go to the **Sources** tab.

    ▪ Click on the line number where you want to pause the execution.

    ▪ When the breakpoint is hit, you can inspect the values and step through your code line by line.

3. **Error Handling and Stack Traces**:

- o When JavaScript encounters an error, it throws an exception, and most browsers display a **stack trace** that shows where the error occurred.
- o Use **try...catch** blocks to handle errors gracefully in your code and prevent the program from crashing.

javascript

```
try {
  let result = someNonExistentFunction();
} catch (error) {
  console.log(error.message); // Outputs:
someNonExistentFunction is not defined
}
```

4. **Using `debugger` Statement**:

- o The `debugger` statement is used to pause the code execution at a specific point and enter the debugger.

javascript

```
function myFunction() {
  let a = 5;
  debugger; // Pauses execution here
  let b = 10;
  console.log(a + b);
}
```

```
myFunction(); // The execution will pause
at the debugger statement
```

- o Once the code hits the `debugger` statement, the browser's developer tools will open, allowing you to inspect variables and step through the code.

Unit Testing in JavaScript

Unit testing involves writing tests to check individual functions or components to ensure they behave as expected. A **unit test** focuses on testing a small piece of functionality in isolation.

1. **What is Unit Testing?**
   - o Unit testing is a way of testing small, isolated parts of your application to verify that they work correctly.
   - o It is usually done using a testing framework that provides methods for defining test cases, asserting expected results, and reporting failures.

2. **Popular Testing Frameworks**:
   - o **Jest**: A JavaScript testing framework that is simple to use and has built-in support for mock functions, assertions, and running tests asynchronously.
   - o **Mocha**: A flexible testing framework that works well with various assertion libraries like Chai.

183

o **Jasmine**: A behavior-driven testing framework with a clean syntax for writing tests.

3. **Writing Unit Tests**:

o The basic structure of a unit test consists of:

- **Arrange**: Set up the conditions or inputs for the function.

- **Act**: Call the function with the provided inputs.

- **Assert**: Check if the output matches the expected result.

Example using **Jest**:

```javascript

function add(a, b) {
  return a + b;
}

// Test case for add function
test('adds 1 + 2 to equal 3', () => {
  expect(add(1, 2)).toBe(3);
});
```

o In this example, the `test` function defines the test case, `expect(add(1, 2))` calls the function being tested, and `toBe(3)` checks that the result is correct.

184

4. **Running Tests**:

  o After writing the tests, you can run them using the command line or integrated test runners in the IDE (like `npm test` for Jest). This will output whether the tests passed or failed.

Real-World Example: Writing Tests for a Form Submission Function

Let's say we have a **form submission function** that checks whether the user has filled out all required fields before submitting the form. We'll write unit tests to validate that the function works correctly.

1. **HTML (index.html)**: Simple form with name and email fields.

```html
html

<!DOCTYPE html>
<html lang="en">
<head>
  <meta charset="UTF-8">
  <meta                    name="viewport"
content="width=device-width,      initial-
scale=1.0">
  <title>Form Submission</title>
</head>
<body>
```

185

```
<h1>Submit Your Info</h1>
<form id="userForm">
  <label for="name">Name:</label>
  <input        type="text"        id="name"
required><br><br>
  <label for="email">Email:</label>
  <input        type="email"        id="email"
required><br><br>
  <button type="submit">Submit</button>
</form>

<script src="script.js"></script>
</body>
</html>
```

2. **JavaScript (script.js)**: The function to validate and submit the form.

```javascript
javascript

function validateForm() {
  let              name              =
document.getElementById('name').value;
  let              email             =
document.getElementById('email').value;
  if (!name || !email) {
    alert("Both fields are required!");
    return    false;    //    Prevent    form
submission
  }
```

186

```
alert("Form submitted successfully!");
return true;
}


// Attach the validateForm function to the
form's submit event
document.getElementById('userForm').addEv
entListener('submit', function(event) {
  event.preventDefault();
  validateForm();
});
```

3. **Unit Test (form.test.js)**: Now let's write a unit test to verify the functionality of the `validateForm` function using Jest.

```
javascript


// form.js (Separate the form validation
logic for testing)
function validateForm(name, email) {
  if (!name || !email) {
    return "Both fields are required!";
  }
  return "Form submitted successfully!";
}


// form.test.js (Unit test)
```

```
test('returns error message if fields are
empty', () => {
  expect(validateForm("",
"test@example.com")).toBe("Both fields are
required!");
  expect(validateForm("Alice",
"")).toBe("Both fields are required!");
});

test('returns success message if fields are
filled', () => {
  expect(validateForm("Alice",
"alice@example.com")).toBe("Form submitted
successfully!");
});
```

How it works:

- **Test Case 1**: We test the case where one or both fields are empty. The expected result is the error message `"Both fields are required!"`.

- **Test Case 2**: We test the case where both fields are filled, and the expected result is the success message `"Form submitted successfully!"`.

4. **Running the Tests**:
   o With Jest installed, you can run the tests by executing `npm test` from the command line. Jest

will run the test cases and output whether they pass or fail.

Summary

In this chapter, we introduced the important concepts of **debugging** and **unit testing** in JavaScript. We learned how to use **debugging techniques** like `console.log()`, breakpoints, and the `debugger` statement to identify and fix issues. We also explored **unit testing** as a method to validate individual functions and components of your code, ensuring they behave as expected. By writing tests for a form submission function, we demonstrated how to use Jest to automate testing and improve code quality. Testing helps ensure that code works as intended and makes it easier to detect and fix issues early in the development process.

CHAPTER 20

PERFORMANCE OPTIMIZATION

Performance is critical in web development, especially as applications grow in complexity and size. Slow performance can significantly affect user experience, making your website or application feel sluggish. In this chapter, we will explore common performance bottlenecks, provide tips for writing efficient JavaScript code, and walk through a real-world example of optimizing a JavaScript-heavy web page.

Common Performance Bottlenecks and How to Avoid Them

1. **Excessive DOM Manipulation**:
   o Manipulating the DOM (Document Object Model) can be costly, especially if you frequently update or manipulate large portions of the page. Each time you interact with the DOM, the browser needs to recalculate the layout, repaint the screen, and possibly reflow elements. This can lead to performance issues if not handled carefully.

   How to avoid it:

190

- o **Batch DOM manipulations**: Instead of making multiple DOM changes one at a time, group them together and update the DOM in a single operation.

- o **Use `documentFragment`**: When adding multiple elements, use `documentFragment` to reduce the number of reflows.

- o **Avoid unnecessary reflows and repaints**: Try to avoid making changes that affect layout or visibility unless necessary.

javascript

```javascript
let fragment = document.createDocumentFragment();
let newElement = document.createElement('div');
newElement.textContent = 'New Element';
fragment.appendChild(newElement);
document.body.appendChild(fragment);
```

2. **Memory Leaks**:

- o Memory leaks occur when objects or data are no longer needed but are not cleared, causing the browser to consume more memory over time. This can result in slower performance and even crashes, especially in long-running web applications.

How to avoid it:

- o **Properly remove event listeners**: If you're adding event listeners dynamically, make sure to remove them when they are no longer needed.
- o **Clean up references**: Make sure to nullify object references when they are no longer needed to help the garbage collector clean up memory.

```javascript
let element = document.getElementById('button');
function onClick() {
  console.log('Button clicked');
}
element.addEventListener('click', onClick);

// Later, remove the event listener
element.removeEventListener('click', onClick);
```

3. **Blocking JavaScript Execution**:
   - o JavaScript runs on a single thread, which means if one part of your code is executing for too long (like a long-running loop or an expensive computation), it can block other operations,

including rendering updates, event handling, and user interaction.

How to avoid it:

- o **Use** **setTimeout** **or** **requestAnimationFrame**: For long-running tasks, break the task into smaller chunks and allow the browser to update the UI or handle user input in between.
- o **Use Web Workers**: Web workers allow you to run JavaScript code in the background on a separate thread, preventing the UI from freezing.

javascript

```
// Using setTimeout to break up a long-
running task
function longRunningTask() {
  let i = 0;
  function doWork() {
    if (i < 10000) {
      console.log(i++);
      setTimeout(doWork, 0); // Allow the
browser to update the UI in between
    }
  }
  doWork();
}
```

193

```
longRunningTask();
```

4. **Unoptimized Loops**:
   - o Loops are often the source of performance issues, especially if they're processing a large amount of data in an inefficient manner.

   How to avoid it:

   - o **Use efficient looping techniques**: Use `for` loops instead of `for...in` or `for...of` when dealing with large datasets, as they are generally faster.
   - o **Cache array length in loops**: In a loop that iterates over an array, store the length in a variable before the loop to avoid recalculating it on each iteration.

   ```javascript
   // Cache the length of the array for
   optimization
   let arr = [1, 2, 3, 4, 5];
   let len = arr.length;
   for (let i = 0; i < len; i++) {
     console.log(arr[i]);
   }
   ```

5. **Overuse of External Libraries**:

194

o While libraries and frameworks can be helpful, overusing them or including unnecessary libraries in your project can add significant overhead, especially if you're only using a small fraction of the library's functionality.

How to avoid it:

o **Use only what you need**: Instead of loading large libraries, consider using smaller, more lightweight alternatives, or even writing custom solutions for simple tasks.

o **Minify and bundle**: When using external libraries, ensure that they are minified and bundled to reduce file size and improve load times.

Tips for Writing Efficient Code

1. **Minimize Reflows and Repaints**:

   o Every time an element is added, removed, or modified, the browser must recalculate the layout (reflow) and repaint the page. Minimize these actions to improve performance.

   o Group DOM changes together and apply styles in bulk rather than one at a time.

2. **Optimize Event Handling**:

o **Event delegation**: Rather than adding individual event listeners to many elements, attach a single event listener to a parent element and handle events for child elements through event delegation. This reduces the number of event listeners and improves performance.

```javascript
document.getElementById('parent').addEven
tListener('click', function(event) {
  if            (event.target            &&
event.target.matches('button.classname'))
{
    console.log('Button clicked!');
  }
});
```

3. **Lazy Loading**:

   o For images, videos, or other heavy assets, use lazy loading to only load the resource when it is needed (e.g., when it becomes visible in the viewport). This reduces initial page load time.

```html
<img    src="image.jpg"    loading="lazy"
alt="Lazy loaded image">
```

4. **Use `requestAnimationFrame` for Animations**:

   o For smooth animations, use `requestAnimationFrame()` rather than `setTimeout()` or `setInterval()`. This allows the browser to synchronize the animation with the screen refresh rate, improving performance.

   javascript

   ```javascript
   function animate() {
     // Perform animation
     requestAnimationFrame(animate); // Call the function recursively for smooth animation
   }
   animate();
   ```

Real-World Example: Optimizing a JavaScript-Heavy Web Page

Let's consider a **JavaScript-heavy web page** that performs multiple operations—fetching data, displaying it, and updating the DOM frequently. Here's how we can optimize such a page:

1. **Problem**: The page makes frequent API calls, updates the DOM with large datasets, and processes data in loops, resulting in poor performance.

2. **Optimized Solution**:

- o **Minimize DOM manipulation** by batching updates.
- o **Use async/await and fetch** to handle HTTP requests efficiently.
- o **Implement virtual DOM** techniques to only update parts of the page that change.
- o **Use `requestAnimationFrame`** for animations or continuous visual updates.

Here's how you might refactor the code:

javascript

```
async function fetchDataAndUpdateDOM() {
  try {
    // Fetch data using async/await
    let response = await
fetch('https://api.example.com/data');
    let data = await response.json();

    // Use document fragment to minimize
DOM updates
    let fragment =
document.createDocumentFragment();
    data.forEach(item => {
      let div =
document.createElement('div');
      div.textContent = item.name;
      fragment.appendChild(div);
```

```
    });

    // Append the fragment to the DOM in a
single operation

document.getElementById('container').appe
ndChild(fragment);
  } catch (error) {
    console.error('Error fetching data:',
error);
  }
}

// Fetch and update the DOM on page load
window.onload = fetchDataAndUpdateDOM;
```

Optimizations made:

- We **batch DOM updates** by using a `documentFragment`, which reduces reflows and repaints.
- We use **async/await** with the Fetch API to handle asynchronous operations in a cleaner, more readable way.
- We limit the **DOM updates to only once** when all data is ready.

Summary

In this chapter, we covered **performance optimization techniques** for JavaScript. We discussed common performance bottlenecks such as excessive DOM manipulation, memory leaks, and inefficient loops, and how to avoid them. We also provided tips for writing efficient code, including minimizing reflows, using event delegation, and optimizing animations with `requestAnimationFrame`. Finally, we demonstrated a real-world example of optimizing a JavaScript-heavy web page by reducing the number of DOM updates and using efficient async operations. By applying these optimization techniques, you can improve the performance of your JavaScript applications, leading to a smoother and faster user experience.

CHAPTER 21

INTRODUCTION TO JAVASCRIPT FRAMEWORKS

JavaScript frameworks provide a structured environment for building web applications. They offer tools, libraries, and patterns that simplify development by providing pre-written code for common tasks. This chapter will explain what **JavaScript frameworks** are, why they are useful, and provide an overview of some of the most popular frameworks like **React**, **Vue**, and **Angular**. Additionally, we will walk through a real-world example of **choosing the right framework for your project**.

What Are Frameworks and Why Use Them?

1. **What is a JavaScript Framework?**

    o A **JavaScript framework** is a pre-built, reusable collection of code that provides a structure for building applications. Unlike a library (which is a collection of functions that you call), a framework dictates the structure and flow of the application, guiding how and when things are done. This **opinionated structure** helps developers focus on the unique aspects of their project without reinventing the wheel.

201

- o Frameworks typically include a set of features, such as:
    - **Routing**: Managing URL routes and loading appropriate views.
    - **State Management**: Managing the application state, such as user inputs, data from APIs, etc.
    - **Templating**: Automatically updating the UI based on the state of the application.
    - **Component-based architecture**: Breaking down the UI into smaller, reusable pieces (components).

2. **Why Use a Framework?**
    - o **Consistency**: Frameworks provide a set of best practices and patterns, ensuring consistency across the codebase, which is especially important in larger teams and projects.
    - o **Speed**: Frameworks come with pre-built solutions for common tasks, such as handling forms, routing, and managing state, reducing the time spent on building these features from scratch.
    - o **Maintenance**: Frameworks are regularly updated and optimized, ensuring better performance, security, and ease of maintenance.

- o **Community Support**: Popular frameworks have large communities and plenty of resources, tutorials, and third-party tools to help developers.
- o **Scalability**: Frameworks are designed to scale well as applications grow, both in terms of performance and maintainability.

Overview of Popular Frameworks

Three of the most popular JavaScript frameworks are **React**, **Vue**, and **Angular**. Let's look at each of them in detail.

1. **React**:
   - o **React** is a **JavaScript library** for building user interfaces, developed by Facebook. Although technically a "library," it is often referred to as a "framework" because it provides a comprehensive set of tools for developing modern, single-page web applications (SPAs).

Key Features:

- o **Component-based architecture**: React applications are made up of small, reusable components that can manage their own state and render the UI.
- o **Virtual DOM**: React uses a virtual DOM to efficiently update only the parts of the UI that

need to be changed, resulting in faster performance.

o **Declarative**: React allows you to describe what the UI should look like, and it handles the rendering and updates automatically.

When to Use:

o React is ideal for building dynamic, high-performance user interfaces, particularly for single-page applications. It's especially useful for projects that require a fast, interactive user interface.

Example:

```javascript
import React, { useState } from 'react';

function Counter() {
  const [count, setCount] = useState(0);

  return (
    <div>
      <p>You clicked {count} times</p>
      <button          onClick={()            =>
setCount(count + 1)}>Click me</button>
    </div>
```

```
    );
}
```

```
export default Counter;
```

2. **Vue**:

   o **Vue.js** is a progressive JavaScript framework for building user interfaces. It is designed to be incrementally adoptable, meaning that you can use as little or as much of it as you need in a project.

Key Features:

   o **Reactivity**: Vue's reactive data binding system makes it easy to keep the UI in sync with the state of the application.

   o **Declarative rendering**: Like React, Vue allows you to declaratively bind data to the DOM and automatically update the DOM when the data changes.

   o **Single-file components**: Vue encourages a component-based architecture, where each component can encapsulate its own template, logic, and style in a single file.

When to Use:

o   Vue is great for small to medium-sized projects where ease of integration and simplicity are key. It's a good choice for developers looking for a lightweight framework with a gentle learning curve.

Example:

```javascript
<template>
  <div>
    <p>You clicked {{ count }} times</p>
    <button        @click="increment">Click
me</button>
  </div>
</template>

<script>
export default {
  data() {
    return {
      count: 0
    };
  },
  methods: {
    increment() {
      this.count++;
    }
```

```
    }
  };
</script>
```

3. **Angular**:

   o **Angular** is a full-fledged, opinionated framework for building web applications, developed by Google. It comes with a complete solution for building SPAs, including routing, state management, form handling, and HTTP client modules.

   Key Features:

   o **Two-way data binding**: Angular's two-way data binding ensures that changes to the model are immediately reflected in the view and vice versa.

   o **Directives**: Angular uses directives to extend HTML with custom attributes and behaviors.

   o **Dependency injection**: Angular's built-in dependency injection system makes it easier to manage services and their dependencies across the application.

   o **RxJS**: Angular leverages **Reactive Programming** (with RxJS) for managing asynchronous operations and event-driven systems.

When to Use:

- o Angular is best suited for large-scale, complex applications where you need a full-featured framework with built-in tools and advanced capabilities. It's commonly used in enterprise-level applications.

Example:

```typescript
import { Component } from '@angular/core';

@Component({
  selector: 'app-counter',
  template: `
    <p>You clicked {{ count }} times</p>
    <button    (click)="increment()">Click me</button>
  `
})
export class CounterComponent {
  count = 0;

  increment() {
    this.count++;
  }
}
```

Real-World Example: Choosing the Right Framework for Your Project

Choosing the right framework depends on several factors such as project size, team expertise, project requirements, and scalability. Let's look at a few scenarios where you might choose each of the three frameworks.

1. **Small Project (Single-Page Application with Minimal Interactivity)**:
   o **Vue** would be a great choice for small to medium-sized projects. It has a gentle learning curve, and you can easily add it to existing projects without major refactoring. If you need to build a simple app with some dynamic elements, Vue provides a straightforward approach without much overhead.

2. **Large-Scale Project (Complex User Interface with High Interactivity)**:
   o **React** is perfect for projects that require a highly dynamic, interactive user interface. Its component-based structure and virtual DOM make it a great choice for building large applications where performance is a concern. It's particularly effective when you need to manage complex state interactions across many UI components.

3. **Enterprise-Level Application (Full-Featured Application with Complex Features)**:

   o **Angular** is well-suited for large-scale, enterprise-level applications where you need a full framework that provides tools for routing, state management, form handling, and HTTP requests out of the box. If your project requires a highly structured architecture, Angular's opinionated nature will help maintain consistency and modularity throughout the application.

Summary

In this chapter, we explored **JavaScript frameworks** and their role in modern web development. We discussed the key features of **React**, **Vue**, and **Angular**, and how each of these frameworks is suited to different types of projects based on size, complexity, and requirements. Choosing the right framework for your project is crucial to ensure scalability, maintainability, and developer productivity. By understanding the strengths of each framework, you can make an informed decision that best suits your project needs.

CHAPTER 22

WORKING WITH REACT.JS

React.js is a powerful JavaScript library for building user interfaces, particularly for single-page applications. It allows developers to create dynamic, interactive UIs with a component-based architecture. In this chapter, we will introduce React.js, explain key concepts like components, JSX, and hooks, and explore how to manage state and props in React. We will also build a simple React-based app to demonstrate how React works in practice.

Introduction to React: Components, JSX, and Hooks

1. **What is React?**

    o   **React** is a declarative, efficient, and flexible JavaScript library for building user interfaces. It was developed by Facebook and has become one of the most widely used libraries for building dynamic web applications.

    o   React allows you to build UIs using **components**, which are reusable pieces of code that manage their own state and rendering logic.

2. **Components**:

- o A **component** in React is a JavaScript function or class that returns a piece of UI. Components can be either **functional** or **class-based**. However, with the introduction of **Hooks** in React 16.8, functional components have become the preferred approach.

Functional Component:

```javascript

function MyComponent() {
  return <h1>Hello, World!</h1>;
}
```

Class-based Component:

```javascript

class MyComponent extends React.Component {
  render() {
    return <h1>Hello, World!</h1>;
  }
}
```

- o Components can also **accept inputs** in the form of **props** and manage their own state using **state**.

3. **JSX (JavaScript XML)**:

- o **JSX** is a syntax extension for JavaScript that allows you to write HTML-like code inside JavaScript. It makes React code easier to write and understand.
- o JSX is then compiled into regular JavaScript code that the browser can execute. For example, `<h1>Hello, World!</h1>` in JSX would be transformed into `React.createElement("h1", null, "Hello, World!")`.

javascript

```javascript
function MyComponent() {
  const name = "Alice";
  return <h1>Hello, {name}!</h1>;  // JSX
}
```

- o JSX is not mandatory, but it is widely used because it is cleaner and more readable.

4. **Hooks**:
  - o **Hooks** are functions that let you "hook into" React features, such as **state** and **lifecycle methods**, from functional components. The most common hooks are `useState` and `useEffect`.
  - o **useState Hook**: Allows you to add state to functional components.

213

```
javascript

import React, { useState } from
'react';

function Counter() {
  const [count, setCount] =
useState(0);

  return (
    <div>
      <p>You clicked {count}
times</p>
      <button onClick={() =>
setCount(count + 1)}>Click
me</button>
    </div>
  );
}
```

o **useEffect Hook**: Allows you to perform side effects, such as fetching data or subscribing to events, in functional components.

```
javascript

import React, { useState, useEffect
} from 'react';
```

214

```
function App() {
  const    [data,      setData]    =
useState(null);

  useEffect(() => {

fetch('https://api.example.com/data
')
      .then(response              =>
response.json())
      .then(data => setData(data));
  }, []);  // The empty array ensures
the effect runs only once

  return <div>{data ? <p>{data}</p>
: <p>Loading...</p>}</div>;
}
```

- o **useEffect** is used here to fetch data when the component mounts. The empty array `[]` as the second argument ensures the effect runs only once, similar to `componentDidMount` in class-based components.

Managing State and Props in React

1. **Props (Properties)**:
   - o **Props** are inputs to a React component, similar to function arguments. They are passed to

components by their parent and are **immutable**, meaning they cannot be changed inside the child component.

javascript

```javascript
function Greeting(props) {
  return <h1>Hello, {props.name}!</h1>;
}
```

```javascript
// Usage
<Greeting name="Alice" />
```

- o In this example, name is a prop passed to the Greeting component, which then displays it inside an <h1> tag.

2. **State**:
   - o **State** is data that can change over time and is managed within the component. Unlike props, which are passed to components from parents, state is managed **locally** within the component using the useState hook (for functional components).

javascript

```javascript
function Counter() {
  const [count, setCount] = useState(0);
```

```
return (
  <div>
    <p>You clicked {count} times</p>
    <button        onClick={()        =>
setCount(count + 1)}>Click me</button>
  </div>
 );
}
```

- o   In this example, `count` is the state, and `setCount` is the function used to update the state. Every time the button is clicked, `setCount` is called, updating the state and causing the component to re-render with the new value.

3. **Props vs. State**:

- o   **Props** are passed to the component and are immutable.

- o   **State** is managed inside the component and is mutable.

- o   Use **props** to pass data down from parent to child components and **state** to manage data that needs to change over time within a component.

Real-World Example: Building a Simple React-Based App

Let's build a simple **React-based app** that allows users to manage a to-do list. This app will demonstrate how to use **state**, **props**, and **hooks** in React.

1. **Setting Up the Project**:
   - If you're using **Create React App** to bootstrap the project, you can set it up with the following command:

   bash

   ```bash
   npx create-react-app todo-app
   cd todo-app
   npm start
   ```

2. **Creating the To-Do List App**:
   - **App Component (App.js)**:

   javascript

   ```javascript
   import React, { useState } from 'react';

   function App() {
     const [tasks, setTasks] = useState([]);
   // State to store tasks
     const [taskInput, setTaskInput] =
   useState('');  // State for input field
   ```

```
const addTask = () => {
  if (taskInput) {
    setTasks([...tasks, taskInput]);
    setTaskInput('');   // Clear input
field
  }
};

const handleInputChange = (event) => {
  setTaskInput(event.target.value);
};

return (
  <div>
    <h1>To-Do List</h1>
    <input
      type="text"
      value={taskInput}
      onChange={handleInputChange}
      placeholder="Add a new task"
    />
    <button       onClick={addTask}>Add
Task</button>
    <ul>
      {tasks.map((task, index) => (
        <li key={index}>{task}</li>
      ))}
    </ul>
```

```
    </div>
  );
}
```

```
export default App;
```

- o **How it works**:
  - The **tasks** state holds an array of tasks.
  - The **taskInput** state is used to bind the input field to the app's state, keeping the input value controlled.
  - When the user types a task and clicks the **Add Task** button, the addTask function is called, which adds the task to the tasks array using setTasks.
  - The tasks are rendered dynamically using the .map() method, displaying each task in an <li> element.

3. **App Structure**:
   - o The application is simple, with a text input field to add tasks and a list to display them.
   - o The state is managed using React's **useState** hook, and props are used implicitly, as data flows from the state to the UI.

Summary

In this chapter, we introduced **React.js**, a powerful JavaScript library for building dynamic user interfaces. We explored key concepts like **components, JSX**, and **hooks**, and explained how to manage **state** and **props** in React components. We also built a real-world example—a simple **to-do list app**—to demonstrate how to use React's features in practice.

React's declarative nature, component-based structure, and hooks like `useState` and `useEffect` make it a powerful tool for building modern web applications. Understanding how to manage state, use props to pass data between components, and leverage hooks will help you build efficient and interactive UIs with React.

CHAPTER 23

INTRODUCTION TO NODE.JS AND EXPRESS

Node.js and Express are fundamental technologies for building modern, server-side JavaScript applications. Node.js allows you to run JavaScript outside the browser, making it possible to build back-end services using JavaScript. Express, a framework built on top of Node.js, simplifies the process of building web applications and APIs. In this chapter, we will explore **Node.js**, set up a simple server, introduce **Express**, and create a real-world example by building a **RESTful API**.

What is Node.js? Setting Up a Node.js Server

1. **What is Node.js?**

   o **Node.js** is a JavaScript runtime built on Chrome's **V8 JavaScript engine**. It allows you to execute JavaScript code on the server side, enabling you to build fast, scalable web applications.

   o **Key Features**:

     ▪ **Asynchronous, event-driven**: Node.js uses an event-driven, non-blocking I/O model, making it lightweight and

222

efficient for handling concurrent requests.

- **Single-threaded**: Node.js runs on a single thread, making it easier to manage resources efficiently.

- **npm (Node Package Manager)**: With npm, Node.js allows you to manage libraries and dependencies easily.

2. **Setting Up a Basic Node.js Server**:

   o To get started with Node.js, you need to have **Node.js** installed on your system. You can download it from the official website.

Steps to Set Up a Basic Node.js Server:

2. **Install Node.js** (if not already installed):

   - Visit the official Node.js website and install the latest stable version.

3. **Initialize a Project**:

   - Create a new directory for your project and run the following command to initialize it:

```bash
bash
```

```
mkdir my-node-app
cd my-node-app
npm init -y
```

This creates a `package.json` file for managing project dependencies.

4. **Create a Basic Server**:
   - In your project directory, create a file named `server.js`.
   - Add the following code to create a basic HTTP server using Node.js's built-in `http` module:

javascript

```javascript
const http = require('http');

const server = http.createServer((req, res) => {
  res.statusCode = 200;
  res.setHeader('Content-Type', 'text/plain');
  res.end('Hello, World!\n');
});

server.listen(3000, '127.0.0.1', () => {
  console.log('Server running at http://127.0.0.1:3000/');
});
```

- This code sets up a basic HTTP server that listens on port 3000. When you access the server, it will respond with "Hello, World!".

5. **Run the Server**:

- In your terminal, run the following command to start the server:

```bash

node server.js
```

- Open your browser and go to http://127.0.0.1:3000/ to see the server in action.

Introduction to Express for Building Web Applications

1. **What is Express?**

   o **Express** is a minimal and flexible **web application framework** for Node.js. It simplifies the process of building web servers and APIs by providing a robust set of features for routing, middleware, template engines, and more.

   o **Key Features**:

      - **Routing**: Define how the application responds to client requests to specific endpoints.

225

JavaScript: From Beginner to Pro

- **Middleware**: Handle requests and responses before or after they reach your routes.
- **Templating**: Use template engines to generate HTML dynamically.
- **RESTful APIs**: Build APIs that follow REST conventions for CRUD operations.

2. **Setting Up Express**:

   o To use Express, you need to install it via npm:

   bash

   ```
   npm install express
   ```

   o **Creating an Express Server**: Replace the server.js code with the following code to create a basic Express server:

   javascript

   ```
   const express = require('express');
   const app = express();

   // Define a route
   app.get('/', (req, res) => {
     res.send('Hello, World from Express!');
   ```

226

```
});

// Start the server
app.listen(3000, () => {
  console.log('Server    running    at
http://localhost:3000/');
});
```

- This sets up an Express server with a single route (/) that responds with a message.
- Run the server:

```bash
```

```
node server.js
```

- Visit `http://localhost:3000/` to see the response.

Real-World Example: Creating a RESTful API with Node.js and Express

Let's build a simple **RESTful API** that allows clients to perform CRUD (Create, Read, Update, Delete) operations on a list of items (e.g., a to-do list).

1. **Setting Up the Project**:

- o In the terminal, create a new directory for the API and initialize it with npm:

bash

```
mkdir todo-api
cd todo-api
npm init -y
```

2. **Install Dependencies**:
   - o Install Express to manage routing and handling HTTP requests:

bash

```
npm install express
```

3. **Create the API**:
   - o Create a `server.js` file and define the routes for the API:

javascript

```
const express = require('express');
const app = express();

// Middleware to parse JSON bodies
app.use(express.json());
```

```javascript
let todos = [
  { id: 1, task: 'Learn JavaScript' },
  { id: 2, task: 'Build a Node.js API' },
];

// GET all todos
app.get('/todos', (req, res) => {
  res.json(todos);
});

// GET a specific todo by ID
app.get('/todos/:id', (req, res) => {
  const todo = todos.find(t => t.id ===
parseInt(req.params.id));
  if              (!todo)              return
res.status(404).send('Todo not found');
  res.json(todo);
});

// POST a new todo
app.post('/todos', (req, res) => {
  const todo = {
    id: todos.length + 1,
    task: req.body.task,
  };
  todos.push(todo);
  res.status(201).json(todo);
});
```

```javascript
// PUT (update) an existing todo by ID
app.put('/todos/:id', (req, res) => {
  const todo = todos.find(t => t.id ===
parseInt(req.params.id));
  if          (!todo)          return
res.status(404).send('Todo not found');

  todo.task = req.body.task;
  res.json(todo);
});


// DELETE a todo by ID
app.delete('/todos/:id', (req, res) => {
  const todoIndex = todos.findIndex(t =>
t.id === parseInt(req.params.id));
  if    (todoIndex    ===    -1)    return
res.status(404).send('Todo not found');

  todos.splice(todoIndex, 1);
  res.status(204).send();
});


// Start the server
app.listen(3000, () => {
  console.log('Server       running       at
http://localhost:3000/');
});
```

4. **Explanation of the Code**:

- o **GET /todos**: Retrieves all to-do items.
- o **GET /todos/:id**: Retrieves a specific to-do item by its ID.
- o **POST /todos**: Creates a new to-do item. The task property is passed in the request body.
- o **PUT /todos/:id**: Updates an existing to-do item. The updated task is passed in the request body.
- o **DELETE /todos/:id**: Deletes a to-do item by its ID.

5. **Running the API**:

- o Start the server:

```bash
```

```
node server.js
```

- o Test the API using tools like **Postman** or **curl**:
  - **GET**:
    http://localhost:3000/todos
  - **POST**: Send a JSON body { "task": "New Task" } to http://localhost:3000/todos
  - **PUT**: Send a JSON body { "task": "Updated Task" } to http://localhost:3000/todos/1

- **DELETE**: Send a `DELETE` request to `http://localhost:3000/todos/1`

Summary

In this chapter, we introduced **Node.js** and **Express**, two powerful technologies for building web servers and APIs in JavaScript. We learned how to set up a basic Node.js server, install and use the Express framework, and build a **RESTful API** for managing a to-do list. Using Express simplifies routing, request handling, and server management, while Node.js enables us to run JavaScript on the server side. With this knowledge, you can build scalable web applications and services using JavaScript, making it possible to use the same language for both the front-end and back-end of your application.

CHAPTER 24

FULL-STACK DEVELOPMENT WITH JAVASCRIPT

Full-stack development refers to building both the **front-end** (the client-side) and **back-end** (the server-side) of a web application. JavaScript, being a versatile language, allows developers to use it for both the front-end and back-end, enabling **full-stack development** using a single language. In this chapter, we will explore how to integrate the front-end and back-end with JavaScript, build a **full-stack CRUD application** using **Node.js** and **React**, and provide next steps for further learning.

Integrating Front-End and Back-End with JavaScript

1. **Front-End with JavaScript (React.js)**:
    o **React.js** is a powerful JavaScript library for building user interfaces. It helps you create dynamic, interactive single-page applications (SPAs) where the user interacts with the UI without refreshing the page.
    o React components manage the UI state and render changes efficiently, making it ideal for front-end development.

2. **Back-End with JavaScript (Node.js and Express)**:

- o **Node.js** is a JavaScript runtime that allows you to run JavaScript on the server side. It enables the creation of server-side applications using JavaScript.

- o **Express** is a minimal and flexible Node.js framework that simplifies the creation of APIs and handling HTTP requests and responses.

- o **MongoDB** is often used as the database for full-stack JavaScript applications, as it works well with JavaScript and stores data in a JSON-like format.

3. **How Full-Stack JavaScript Works Together**:

- o The **front-end** (React.js) communicates with the **back-end** (Node.js/Express) using **HTTP requests**, typically in the form of **RESTful API calls**. These requests are made using **fetch** or **axios** (a popular HTTP client library for JavaScript).

- o The **back-end** handles these requests, interacts with the database, and returns the data to the front-end for display.

Real-World Example: Building a Full-Stack CRUD Application

In this example, we will build a **full-stack CRUD (Create, Read, Update, Delete) application** where users can add, view, update, and delete notes.

Tools and Libraries Used:

- **Front-End**: React.js for the user interface.
- **Back-End**: Node.js and Express for the server-side logic.
- **Database**: MongoDB to store notes data.
- **HTTP Requests**: Axios to communicate between the front-end and back-end.

Step 1: Setting Up the Back-End (Node.js and Express)

1. **Initialize a Node.js project**:

```bash
mkdir fullstack-crud-app
cd fullstack-crud-app
npm init -y
npm install express mongoose cors
```

2. **Create the back-end structure**: Inside the project directory, create the following structure:

```bash
/backend
  /models
    Note.js
  /routes
```

235

```
notes.js
server.js
```

3. Create the Note model (models/Note.js):

```javascript
const mongoose = require('mongoose');

const noteSchema = new mongoose.Schema({
  title: { type: String, required: true },
  content: { type: String, required: true
},
});

const    Note    =    mongoose.model('Note',
noteSchema);
module.exports = Note;
```

4. Create routes for CRUD operations (routes/notes.js):

```javascript
const express = require('express');
const router = express.Router();
const Note = require('../models/Note');

// Create a new note
router.post('/', async (req, res) => {
  const { title, content } = req.body;
```

```
  const note = new Note({ title, content
});
  try {
    await note.save();
    res.status(201).json(note);
  } catch (err) {
    res.status(400).json({        message:
err.message });
  }
});


// Get all notes
router.get('/', async (req, res) => {
  try {
    const notes = await Note.find();
    res.json(notes);
  } catch (err) {
    res.status(500).json({        message:
err.message });
  }
});


// Update a note
router.put('/:id', async (req, res) => {
  try {
    const       note       =       await
Note.findById(req.params.id);
```

```javascript
    if          (!note)          return
res.status(404).json({ message: 'Note not
found' });

    note.title   =   req.body.title   ||
note.title;
    note.content = req.body.content   ||
note.content;
    await note.save();
    res.json(note);
  } catch (err) {
    res.status(400).json({          message:
err.message });
  }
});

// Delete a note
router.delete('/:id', async (req, res) =>
{
  try {
    const      note      =          await
Note.findById(req.params.id);
    if          (!note)          return
res.status(404).json({ message: 'Note not
found' });

    await note.remove();
    res.json({ message: 'Note deleted' });
  } catch (err) {
```

```
    res.status(500).json({          message:
err.message });
  }
});
```

```
module.exports = router;
```

5. Create the server (server.js):

```javascript
const express = require('express');
const mongoose = require('mongoose');
const cors = require('cors');
const          notesRouter          =
require('./routes/notes');

const app = express();
app.use(cors());
app.use(express.json());

mongoose.connect('mongodb://localhost:270
17/notesdb', {
  useNewUrlParser: true,
  useUnifiedTopology: true,
});

app.use('/api/notes', notesRouter);

const port = 5000;
```

```
app.listen(port, () => {
  console.log(`Server          running          at
http://localhost:${port}`);
});
```

6. **Run the back-end**:

```bash
bash
```

```
node server.js
```

Step 2: Setting Up the Front-End (React)

1. **Create the React app**:

```bash
bash
```

```
npx create-react-app frontend
cd frontend
npm install axios
```

2. **Create the To-Do list UI (App.js)**:

```javascript
javascript
```

```javascript
import React, { useState, useEffect } from
'react';
import axios from 'axios';

function App() {
```

```javascript
const [notes, setNotes] = useState([]);
const [newNote, setNewNote] = useState({
title: '', content: '' });

// Fetch notes from the API
useEffect(() => {

axios.get('http://localhost:5000/api/note
s')
    .then((response)                  =>
setNotes(response.data))
    .catch((error)                    =>
console.error('Error   fetching   notes:',
error));
}, []);

// Handle input change
const handleInputChange = (e) => {
  setNewNote({
    ...newNote,
    [e.target.name]: e.target.value,
  });
};

// Submit new note
const handleSubmit = (e) => {
  e.preventDefault();
```

241

```javascript
axios.post('http://localhost:5000/api/not
es', newNote)
    .then((response)                    =>
setNotes([...notes, response.data]))
    .catch((error)                      =>
console.error('Error     adding     note:',
error));
  };

  return (
    <div>
      <h1>React Full-Stack CRUD App</h1>
      <form onSubmit={handleSubmit}>
        <input
          type="text"
          name="title"
          value={newNote.title}
          onChange={handleInputChange}
          placeholder="Title"
        />
        <textarea
          name="content"
          value={newNote.content}
          onChange={handleInputChange}
          placeholder="Content"
        />
        <button          type="submit">Add
Note</button>
```

242

```
    </form>
    <ul>
      {notes.map((note) => (
        <li key={note._id}>
          <h2>{note.title}</h2>
          <p>{note.content}</p>
        </li>
      ))}
    </ul>
  </div>
  );
}


export default App;
```

3. **Run the Front-End**:

```bash
bash
```

```
npm start
```

Step 3: Testing the Application

- Open the front-end in your browser at http://localhost:3000/.
- Add new notes, view them, and see how they persist by interacting with the back-end API.

Conclusion and Next Steps for Further Learning

In this chapter, we built a **full-stack CRUD application** using **Node.js**, **Express**, and **React**. This app allows users to create, view, update, and delete notes. We learned how to:

- Set up a Node.js server and create a RESTful API with Express.
- Use React for building the front-end, including handling user input and interacting with the back-end.
- Use `axios` to make HTTP requests from the front-end to the back-end.

Next steps for further learning include:

- Learning about **authentication** and **authorization** in full-stack applications.
- Exploring **state management** in React (e.g., using Redux or Context API).
- Implementing **advanced features** like file uploads or real-time updates using **WebSockets**.

www.ingramcontent.com/pod-product-compliance
Lightning Source LLC
LaVergne TN
LVHW022339060326
832902LV00022B/4139